THE WELLINGTON BOOK.

Jess Lunnon
Sandi Mackechnie
Nigel Beckford
Michael Fitzsimons

THE WELLINGTON BOOK

Published 2011 by FitzBeck Publishing
www.thewellingtonbook.co.nz

Contact
Tel: 04 8019669
PO Box 6273, Te Aro, Wellington 6011

ISBN
978-0-473-18698-2

THIS BOOK IS DEDICATED TO WELLINGTONIANS EVERYWHERE, THE STAYERS AND THE ROAMERS. AND TO VISITORS FROM FAR AND WIDE, WELCOME TO OUR CITY.

Kapiti Island
Mt Kaukau
Khandallah.
Ngaio
Karori
Wadestown.
The Terrace
Makara Valley
Aro Valley
Brooklyn
Lambton Quay
Cuba Street
TE PAPA
TOOT!!
Happy Valley
Town Belt
Newtown
Hataitai
Kilbirnie
Rongotai
Red Rocks
Lyall Bay
Moa Point
Island Bay

Johnsonville
Broadmeadows.
Ngauranga Gorge
Hutt
Petone
WELLINGTON
Somes Island
Karaka Bays.
Days Bay
Eastbourne
Seatoun
interislander
Pencarrow Head
N
W
E
S

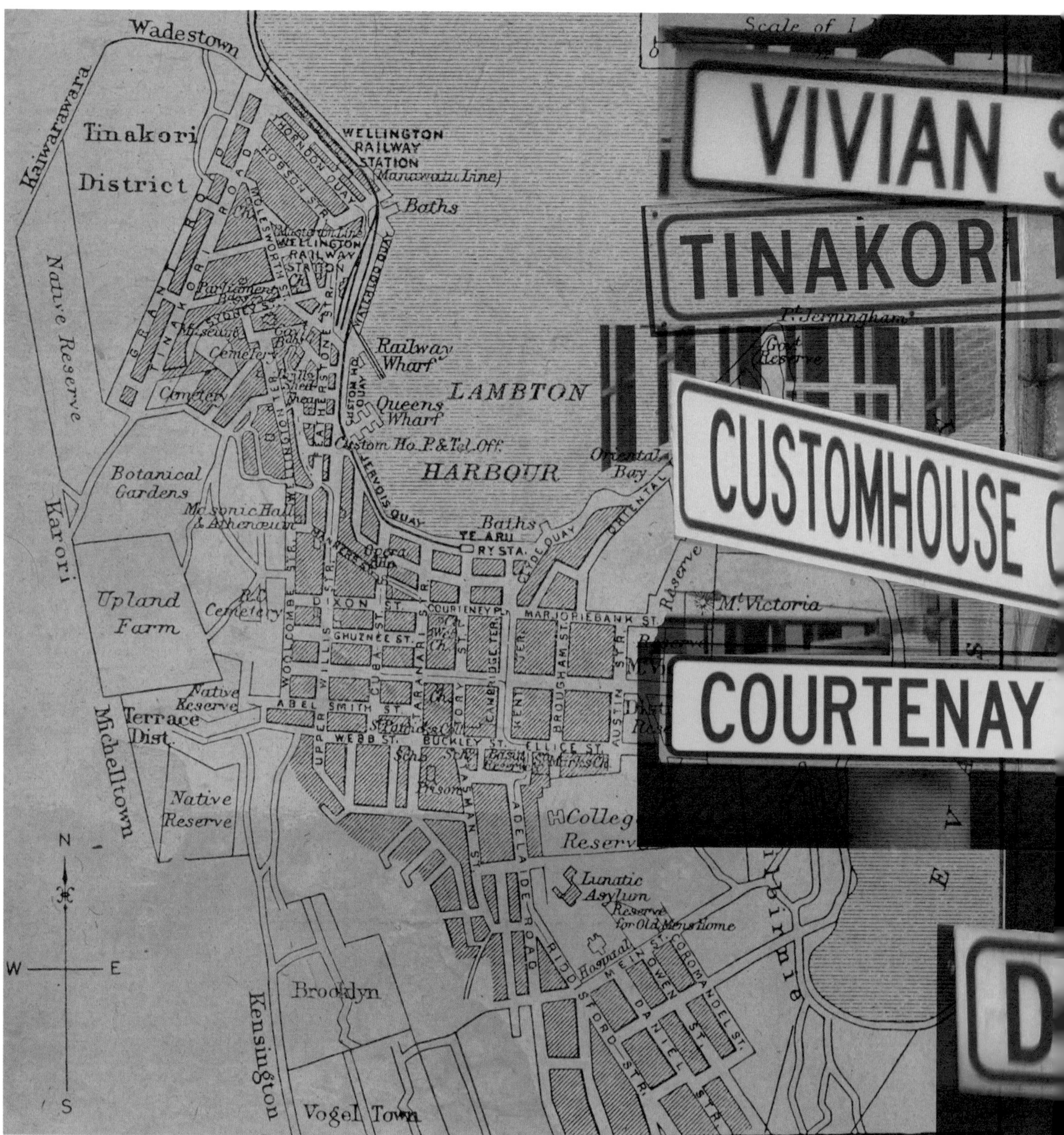

Wadestown
Kaiwarawara
Tinakori
District
Native Reserve
Karori
Botanical Gardens
Upland Farm
WELLINGTON RAILWAY STATION (Manawatu Line)
Baths
Railway Wharf
LAMBTON
Queens Wharf
HARBOUR
Oriental Bay
Mt. Victoria
Native Reserve
Terrace Dist.
Michelltown
Native Reserve
College Reserve
Lunatic Asylum
Reserve for Old Mens Home
Hospital
Brooklyn
Kensington
Vogel Town
N
W
E
S
VIVIAN
TINAKORI
CUSTOMHOUSE
COURTENAY

LAMBTON QUAY
LIMMER STEPS
MARJORIBANKS ST
TARANAKI ST
WILLIS ST
WAKEFIELD ST
CUBA ST
TORY ST
ON ST
GHUZNEE ST

Oriental Parade is named
after one of the first ships
to bring settlers to Wellington.
Home to the Carter Fountain,
it is one of the most
expensive strips of real estate
in New Zealand. A new beach was
created in 2004 when over 27,000
tonnes of sand was barged in from
Takaka in the South Island. It was
completed at a cost of $7.5 million.
The golden sand deposit is replenished
at regular intervals. Oriental Bay is one of
the city's favourite promenades.
Oriental Parade

THE SWEETEST PART

ACCORDING TO MĀORI MYTHOLOGY, MĀUI FISHED UP THE NORTH ISLAND (TE IKA-A-MĀUI). HE WAS SEATED IN HIS SOUTH ISLAND CANOE (TE WAKA A MĀUI) AT THE TIME. THE WELLINGTON REGION WAS IDENTIFIED AS THE HEAD OF MĀUI'S FISH (TE UPOKO O TE IKA A MAUI), THE SWEETEST PART. MĀORI HAVE LIVED IN THE WELLINGTON REGION SINCE THE 10TH CENTURY.

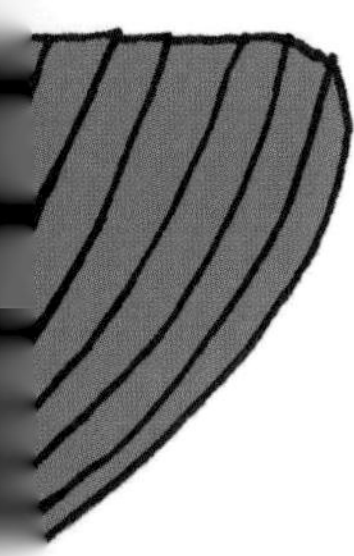

POLYNESIAN VOYAGERS KUPE AND NGAHUE ARE CREDITED WITH THE FIRST DISCOVERY OF WELLINGTON WHEN THEY CAMPED AT THE SOUTHERN END OF THE HARBOUR MORE THAN 1000 YEARS AGO. THE PALLISER BAY AREA AND KAPITI ISLAND CONTAIN SOME OF THE OLDEST RECORDED MĀORI SITES IN NEW ZEALAND.

EUROPEAN
SETTLERS
Shoreline
1840

EUROPEANS BEGAN TO ARRIVE IN WELLINGTON AT THE BEGINNING OF THE

19th CENTURY.

THE NEW ZEALAND COMPANY SETTLERS SAILED INTO WELLINGTON ON THE TORY IN 1839 AND THE AURORA IN 1840. THEY INITIALLY SETTLED IN PETONE BUT FLOODING IN THE AREA CAUSED THEM TO MOVE ACROSS THE HARBOUR.

WITH JUST 5,000 RESIDENTS, WELLINGTON BECAME THE CAPITAL CITY

IN 1865, REPLACING AUCKLAND.

The first Parliament in Wellington was convened in 1862.

THE CITY IS NAMED AFTER THE FIRST DUKE OF WELLINGTON, ARTHUR WELLESLEY, THE VICTOR OF THE BATTLE OF WATERLOO.

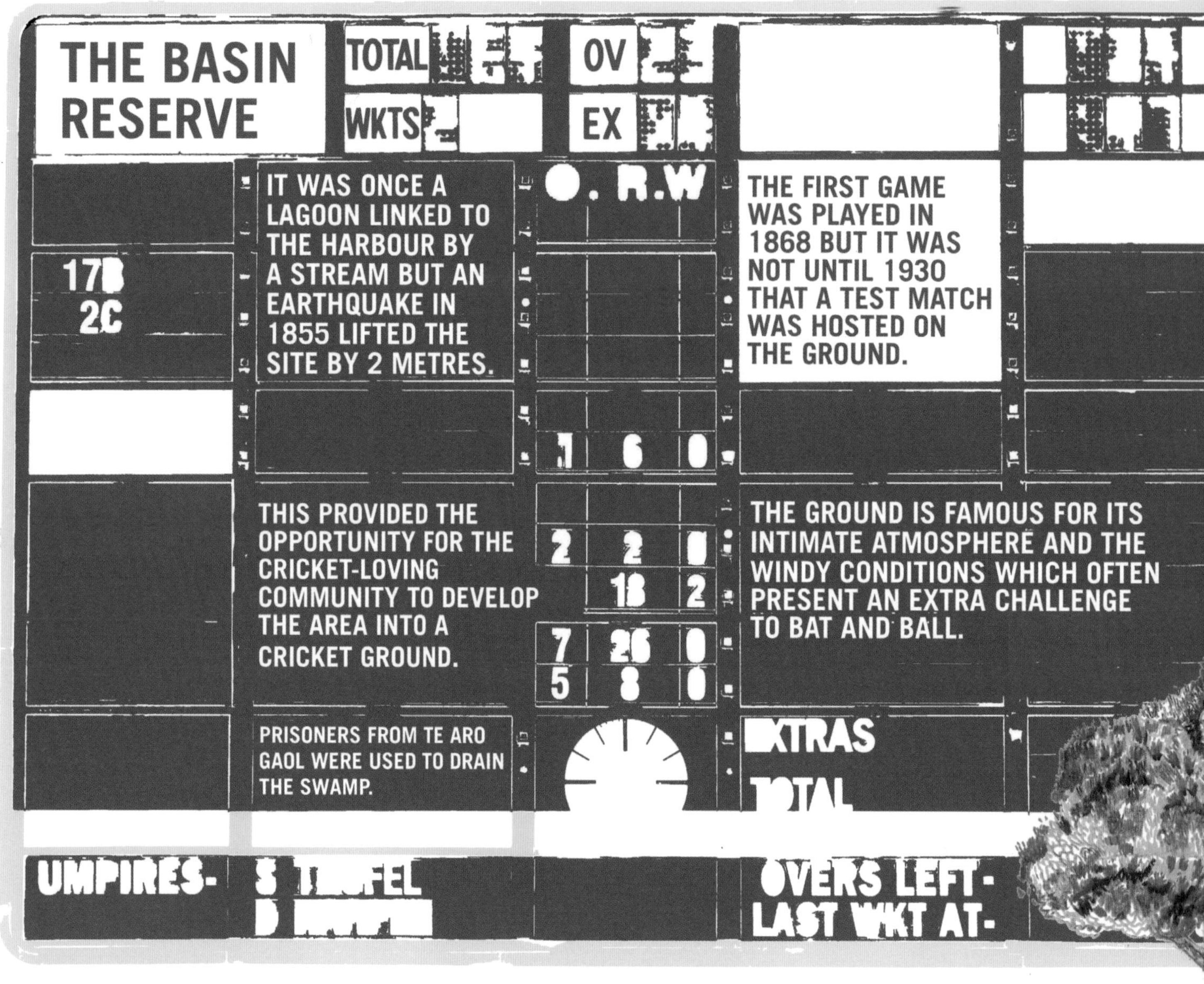

THE BASIN RESERVE IS THE OLDEST FIRST-CLASS CRICKET GROUND IN NZ AND ARGUABLY THE MOST FAMOUS.

THE Basin RESERVE
NZ
AUS

THE "GOLDEN" MILE

THE GOLDEN MILE IS WELLINGTON'S BUSIEST & MOST SOUGHT-AFTER RETAIL LOCATION.

THIS CONTINUOUS STRETCH OF UP-MARKET SHOPS AND HIGH RISE OFFICES RUNS FROM LAMBTON QUAY, NEAR PARLIAMENT THROUGH TO WILLIS STREET.
LAMBTON QUAY WAS ONCE THE FORESHORE OF WELLINGTON UNTIL AN EARTHQUAKE IN 1855 RAISED MORE LAND NEARBY.
MLC
WILLIS ST
Est-1863
KIRKCALDIE & STAINS Ltd
Shoreline
1840
50% OFF
SALE
LAMBTON QUAY
Sale
Sale
Sale
SALE!!

THE WORLD'S SOUTHERNMOST CAPITAL

42°

THE RIVERS
OF WIND

WELLINGTON IS ONE OF THE WORLD'S
(THREE) MOST WINDY CITIES, ALONGSIDE CAPE TOWN, SOUTH AFRICA & REYKJAVIK, ICELAND.
THE AVERAGE WINDSPEED IS (22) Km/h BUT
POWERFUL GUSTS OF MORE THAN (60) Km/h BLAST THE CITY
173 DAYS A year.
THE GALE FORCE WINDS THAT POUND
WELLINGTON OFTEN PEAK OVER (140) Km/h COMPARABLE
TO A MAJOR HURRICANE.
THE STRONGEST
WIND GUST EVER RECORDED WAS
248 KM/HR IN 1959 and 1962.

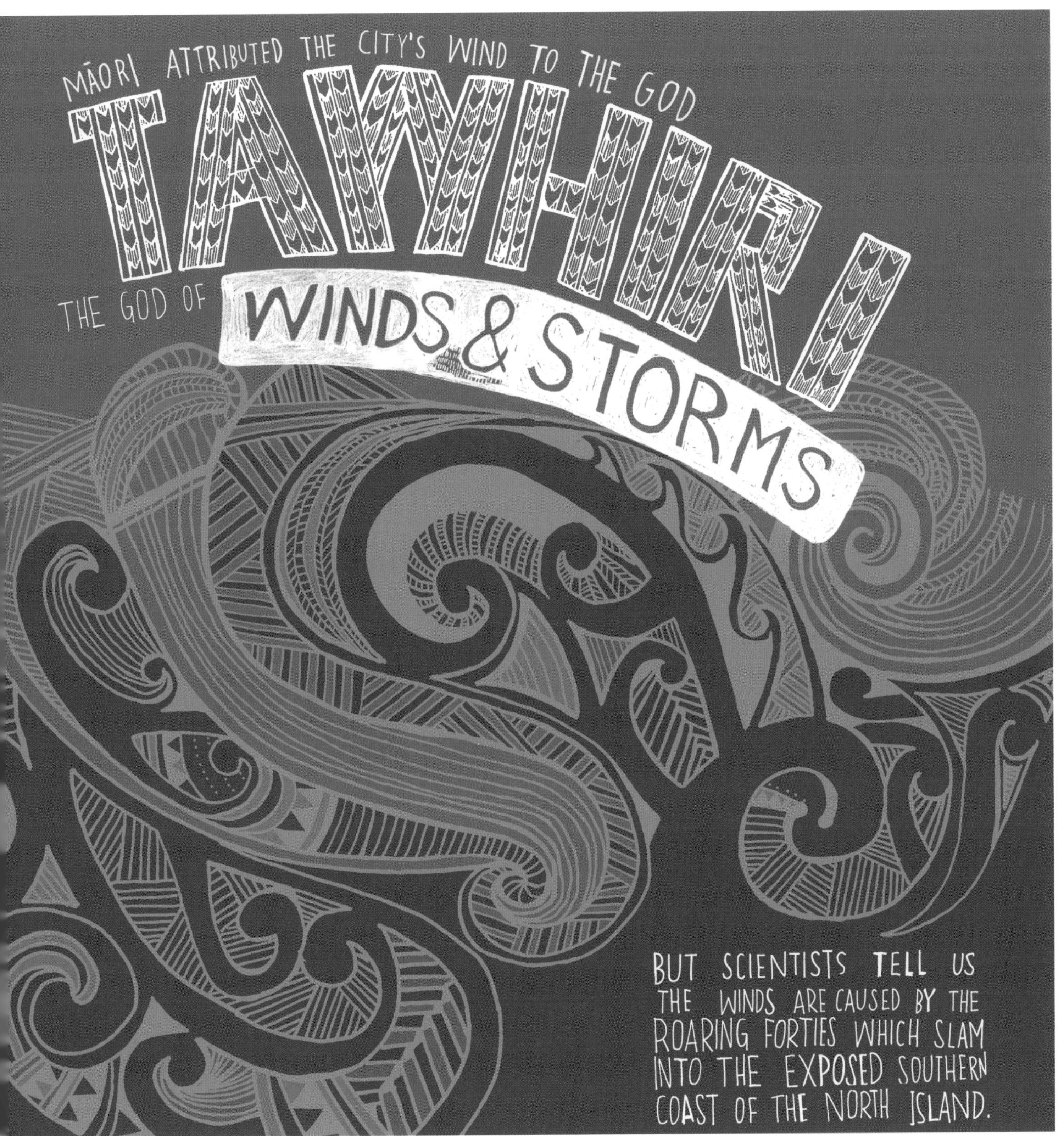
MĀORI ATTRIBUTED THE CITY'S WIND TO THE GOD
TAWHIRI
THE GOD OF WINDS & STORMS
BUT SCIENTISTS TELL US THE WINDS ARE CAUSED BY THE ROARING FORTIES WHICH SLAM INTO THE EXPOSED SOUTHERN COAST OF THE NORTH ISLAND.

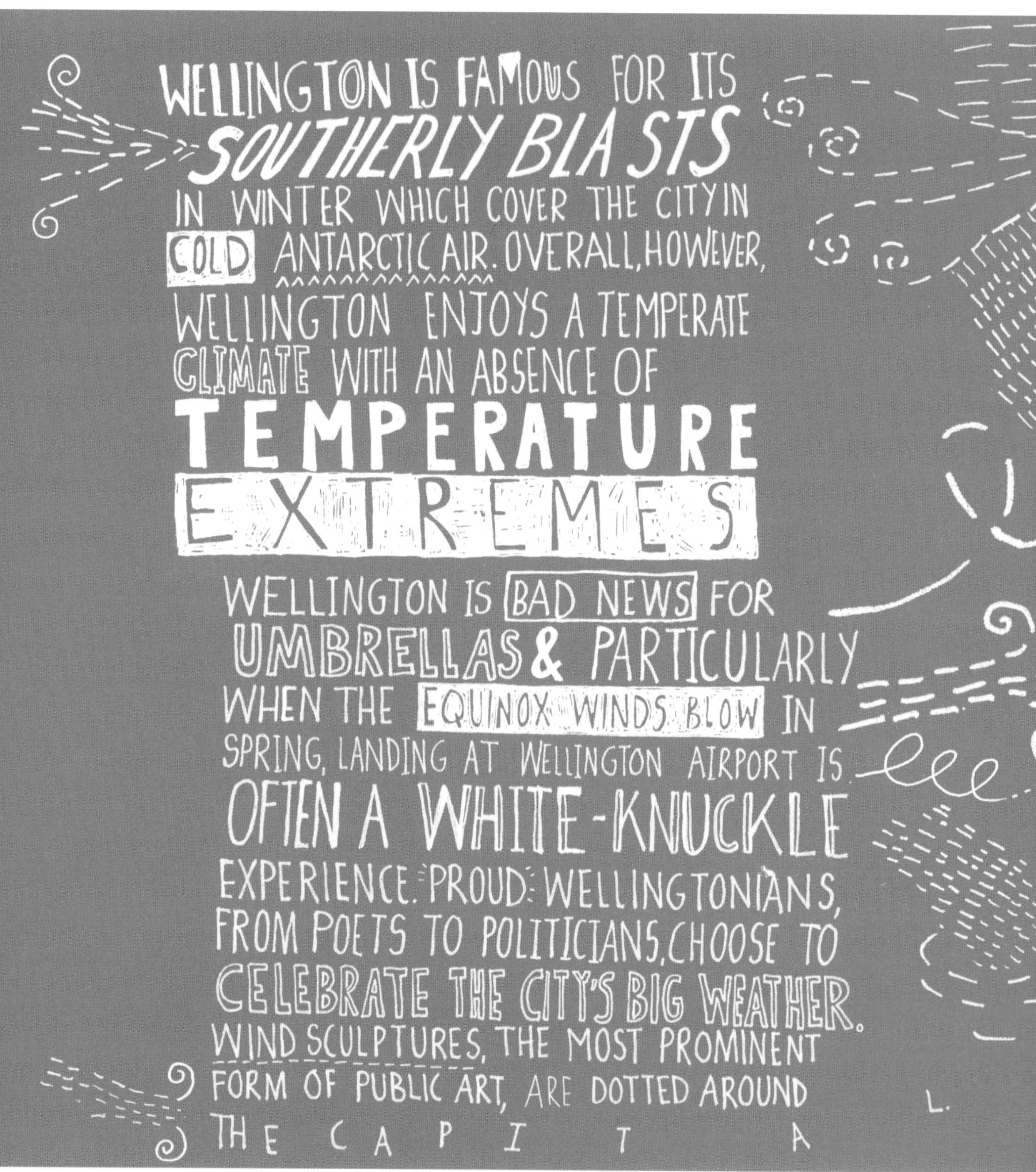
WELLINGTON IS FAMOUS FOR ITS
SOUTHERLY BLASTS
IN WINTER WHICH COVER THE CITY IN
COLD ANTARCTIC AIR. OVERALL, HOWEVER,
WELLINGTON ENJOYS A TEMPERATE
CLIMATE WITH AN ABSENCE OF
TEMPERATURE
EXTREMES
WELLINGTON IS BAD NEWS FOR
UMBRELLAS & PARTICULARLY
WHEN THE EQUINOX WINDS BLOW IN
SPRING, LANDING AT WELLINGTON AIRPORT IS
OFTEN A WHITE-KNUCKLE
EXPERIENCE. PROUD WELLINGTONIANS,
FROM POETS TO POLITICIANS, CHOOSE TO
CELEBRATE THE CITY'S BIG WEATHER.
WIND SCULPTURES, THE MOST PROMINENT
FORM OF PUBLIC ART, ARE DOTTED AROUND
THE CAPITA
L.

DOM
POST

CIVIC SQUARE
CIVIC SQUARE IS A SHELTERED PUBLIC SPACE IN THE HEART OF THE WELLINGTON CBD. THE TERRACOTTA BRICK SQUARE, COMPLETED IN 1992, IS LINED BY CHARACTER PUBLIC BUILDINGS SUCH AS THE TOWN HALL, THE CITY GALLERY, WELLINGTON LIBRARY AND THE MICHAEL FOWLER CENTRE. A PEDESTRIAN BRIDGE AT ONE END OF THE SQUARE ENABLES WELLINGTONIANS TO ACCESS THE WATERFRONT. WORKERS FROM SURROUNDING OFFICES DO SO IN DROVES EVERY LUNCH TIME, ESPECIALLY IN SUMMER.

The Beehive

OUR SEAT OF GOVERNMENT LOOKS MORE LIKE A HAT.

THE BEEHIVE IS THE NICKNAME FOR NEW ZEALAND'S PARLIAMENT. IT WAS DESIGNED BY SCOTTISH ARCHITECT SIR BASIL SPENCE AND WAS COMPLETED IN 1981. IT IS 10 STORIES HIGH AND HAS 4 STORIES BELOW GROUND. THE ROOF IS CONSTRUCTED FROM 20 TONNES OF COPPER. THE PRIME-MINISTER'S OFFICE IS ON THE NINTH FLOOR.

ALL MANNER OF CHERISHED JUNK CAN BE FOUND IN THIS ECCENTRIC SCULPTURE PARK SITUATED DEEP IN HAPPY VALLEY ROAD, BROOKLYN. HUGE ROCKS SIT ALONG SIDE METALLIC SPIDERS, BIRDS, SNAKES AND DOGS. A UNIQUELY ORGANIC 18-HOLE MINI GOLF COURSE COMPLETES THE QUIRKY ENTERTAINMENT.

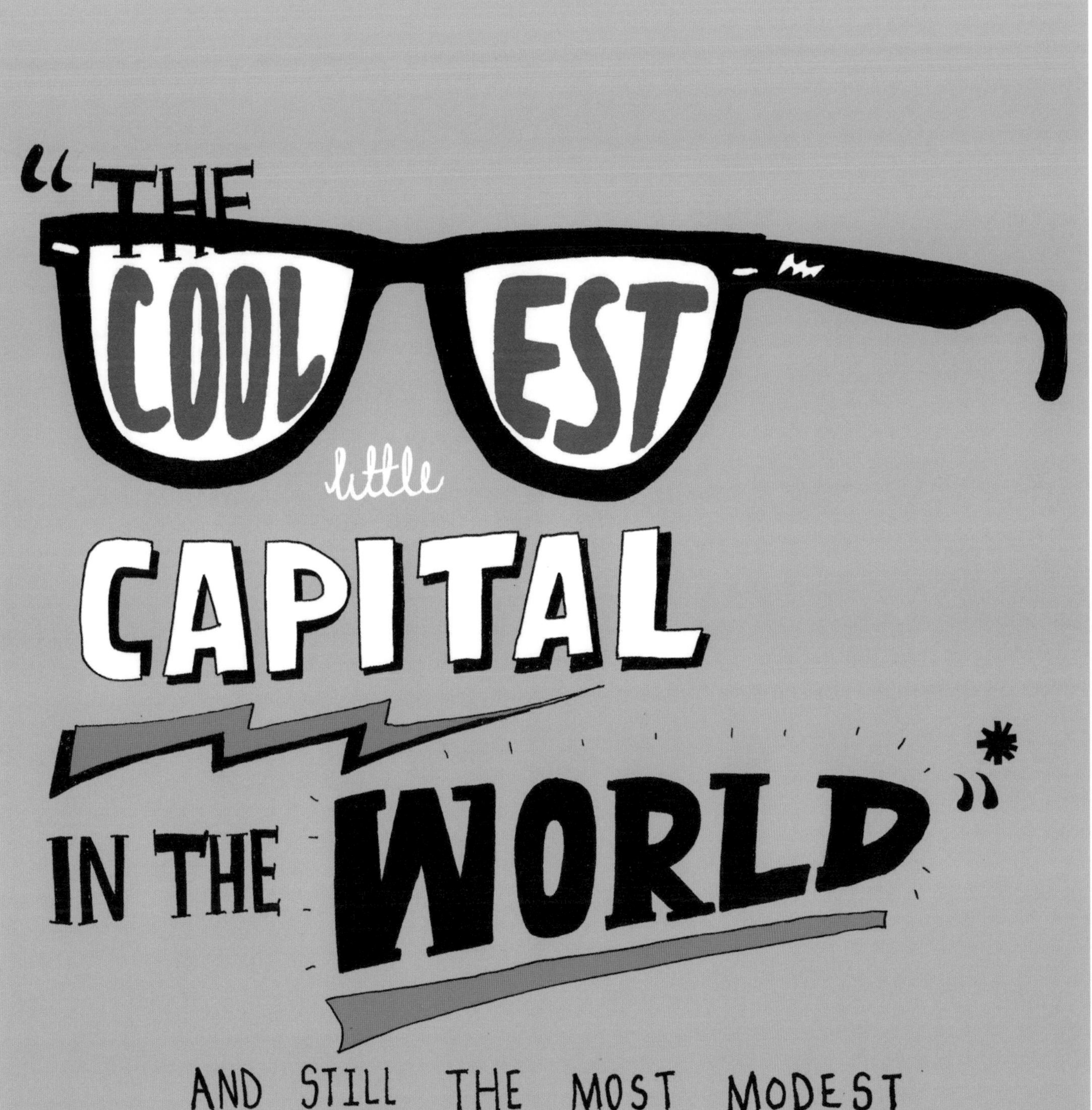
"THE
COOL EST
little
CAPITAL
IN THE WORLD"*
AND STILL THE MOST MODEST
* Lonely Planet 2011

More cafes per capita than New York city.

6 am

8·30am

10·30 am

12·05 pm

2·15 pm

4·20 pm

8·25 pm

ISTRETTO
AMERICHANO
SHORT BLACK
PICCOLO LATTE
CAPPUCCINO
EFFOGATO
CHAI
LATTE MACCHIATO
ESPRESSO
ICED COFFEE
MOCHA
LATTE
CAFE
ONG BLACK
MACCHIATO
FLAT WHITE
HOT CHOC

THE BIRD SONG OF KAPITI ISLAND

NATURE RESERVE

THIS POPULAR MARINE RESERVE + NATIVE SANCTUARY
LIES 5KM OFF THE KAPITI COAST. THE island is the SUMMIT
of a SUBMERGED MOUNTAIN RANGE CREATED BY
EARTHQUAKES 200 MILLION YEARS AGO. KAPITI WAS
HOME to A succession OF MAORI TRIBES IN
PRE-EUROPEAN TIMES, MOST NOTABLY LEGENDARY WARRIOR
TE RAUPARAHA, WHO MADE THE ISLAND HIS STRONGHOLD. IT ALSO
served as a base FOR WHALERS UNTIL THE MID C19th.
TO Keep the island Pest-free, PRIVATE BOATS ARE
NOT PERMITTED to land + ALL VISITORS require a
DEPARTMENT of Conservation ACCESS PERMIT.

AIR NEW ZEALAND
C-FCPO
Welcome to Wellington!

ARMY
ARMY

Wellington's BIGGEST PARTY

THE IRB RUGBY SEVENS IS A HIGHLIGHT OF THE CITY'S SUMMER SPORTING & SOCIAL CALENDAR. MORE THAN 70,000 FANS MANY IN OUTLANDISH FANCY DRESS, FLOCK TO WESTPAC STADIUM FOR THE TWO-DAY EVENT. THE TOURNAMENT IS THE THIRD IN THE IRB WORLD SERIES THAT FEATURES SIXTEEN INTERNATIONAL TEAMS. TICKETS FOR THE ANNUAL EVENT **SELL OUT** IN A MATTER OF MINUTES AND THE CITY HOSTS A MARDI GRAS-LIKE STREET PARADE IN ITS HONOUR.

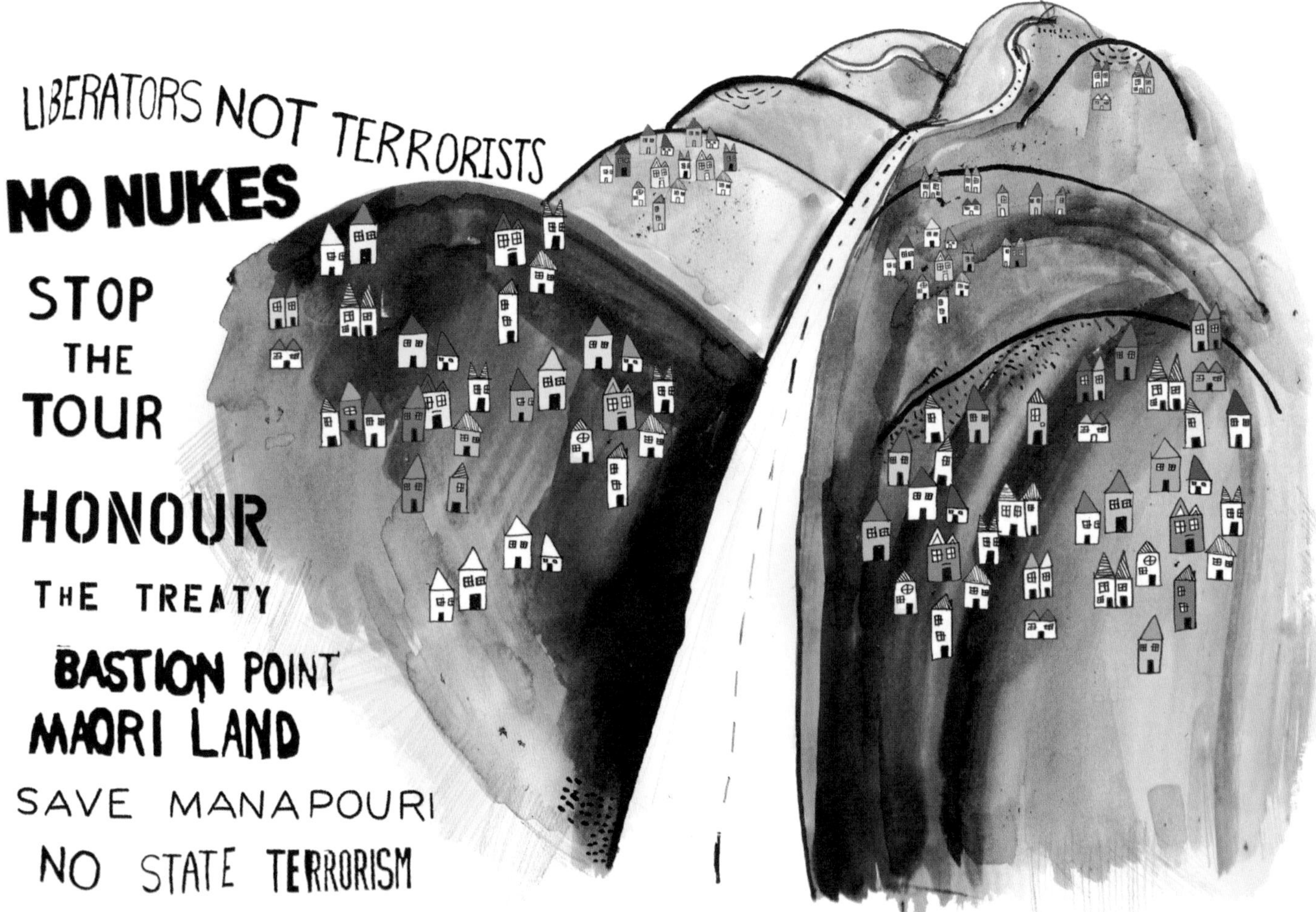
LIBERATORS NOT TERRORISTS
NO NUKES
STOP THE TOUR
HONOUR THE TREATY
BASTION POINT
MAORI LAND
SAVE MANAPOURI
NO STATE TERRORISM
WAIHOPAI SPY
FASHION STINKS
especially when it's made in sweatshops
RESISTANCE is NOT FUTILE
ARO VALLEY

THE HISTORIC ARO VALLEY TAKES ITS NAME FROM A STREAM THAT ONCE FLOWED THROUGH IT. NINETEENTH CENTURY WOOD AND CORRUGATED IRON WORKERS' COTTAGES STILL IMBUE THE INNER CITY SUBURB WITH CHARM AND CHARACTER. IN THE 1960s AND 70s THE VALLEY EARNED A REPUTATION FOR THE RADICALISM OF ITS STUDENT POPULATION AND DESPITE SUBSEQUENT DECADES OF GENTRIFICATION, IT REMAINS A BASTION OF BOHEMIA AND COUNTER CULTURE.

interislander
Bounty
90J516
47620
ISLAND BAY
BLESSING OF THE BOATS

Each year in spring Wellington's Italian community invokes the power of God to look after its fishing fleet and keep its fishermen safe. The 'blessing of the boats' tradition originates in southern Italy, where most of Island Bay's Italian immigrants come from. The famous island in the middle of the bay, Tapu Te Ranga Matu, provides a natural shelter for the fleet.

LesMILLS
AIR NEW ZEALAND
McDonald's
ami ami
YELLOW FEVER
PHOENIX
SONY
20
17

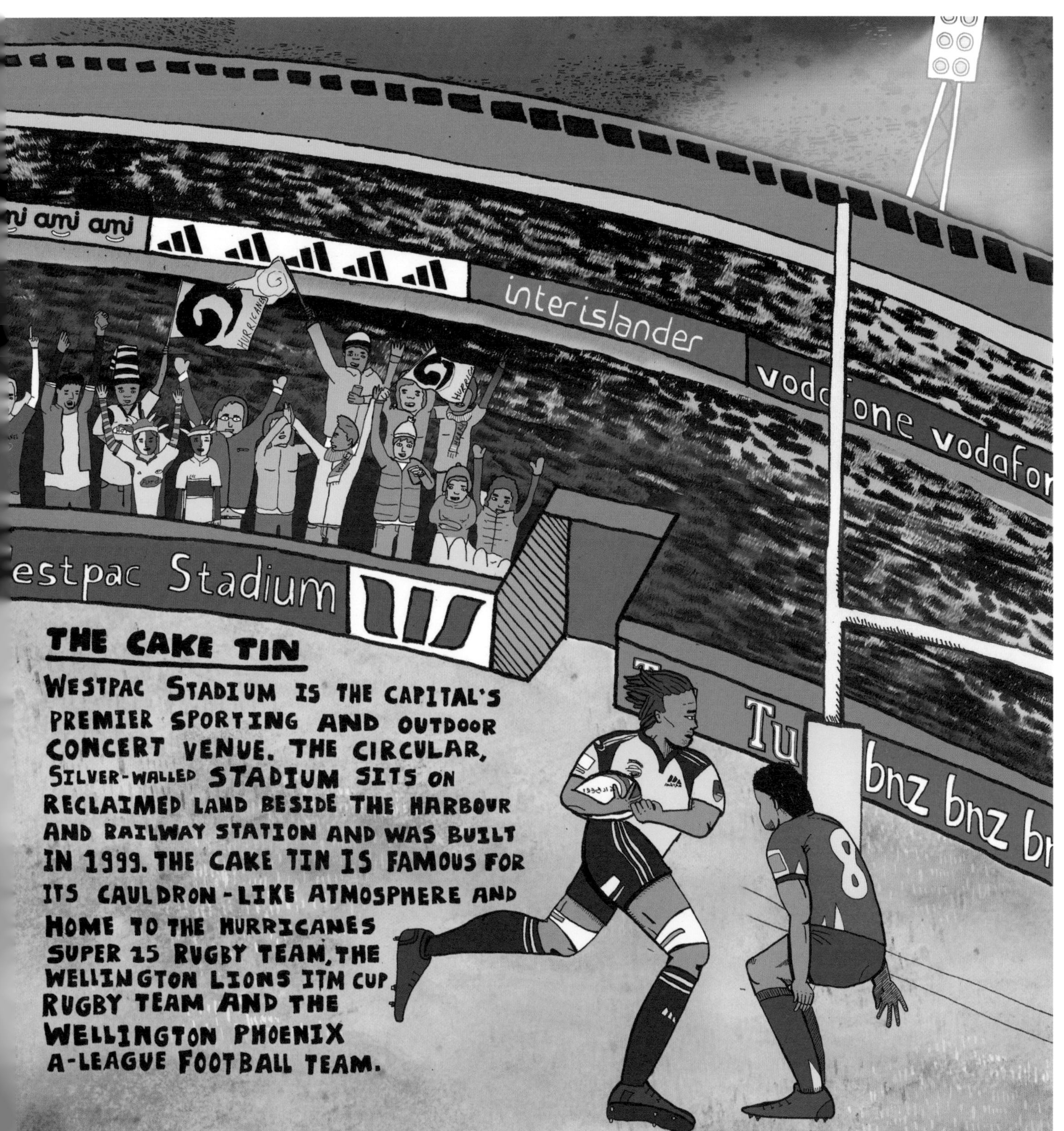

ami ami ami
interislander
vod one vodafor
HURRICANES
estpac Stadium
Tu
bnz bnz br
THE CAKE TIN
WESTPAC STADIUM IS THE CAPITAL'S PREMIER SPORTING AND OUTDOOR CONCERT VENUE. THE CIRCULAR, SILVER-WALLED STADIUM SITS ON RECLAIMED LAND BESIDE THE HARBOUR AND RAILWAY STATION AND WAS BUILT IN 1999. THE CAKE TIN IS FAMOUS FOR ITS CAULDRON-LIKE ATMOSPHERE AND HOME TO THE HURRICANES SUPER 15 RUGBY TEAM, THE WELLINGTON LIONS ITM CUP RUGBY TEAM AND THE WELLINGTON PHOENIX A-LEAGUE FOOTBALL TEAM.

LOCAL LANDMARKS
PLIMMER HOUSE
STATUE OF QUEEN VICTORIA
ST MARY OF THE ANGELS
THE CARILLON - NATIONAL WAR MEMORIAL
ST PETER'S
OLD ST PAUL'S
GOVERNMENT HOUSE

UNITY
BOOKS
WOW
WORLD OF WEARABLE ARTS.
NZ
SYMPHONY
ORCHESTRA
PARSONS

WHAT TIME DOES THE DANCING START IN THIS TOWN?

WELLINGTON'S NIGHTLIFE IS LEGENDARY, LATE AND OFTEN LEGLESS. A COMPACT CENTRAL CITY MEANS EVERY WATERING HOLE IS WITHIN EASY WALKING OR STAGGERING DISTANCE. COURTENAY PLACE HAS EVOLVED INTO A BOISTEROUS, ALL AGES PARTY DESTINATION, WHILE COOLER CATS AND KITTENS HEAD FOR THE PRICIER BOUTIQUE BARS OF THE CUBA QUARTER AND ADJACENT ALLEYWAYS.

BE COOL!

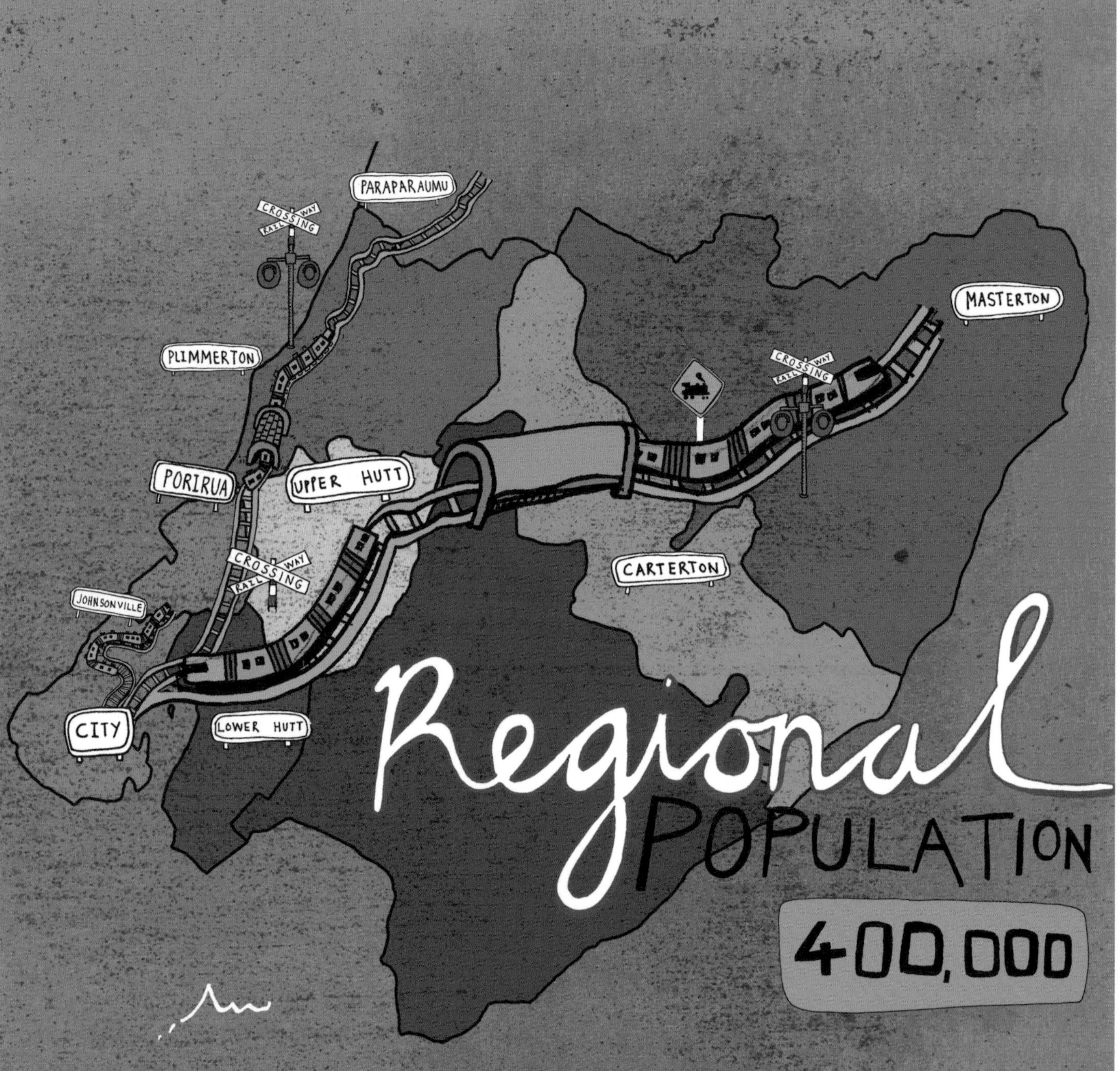
PARAPARAUMU
RAILWAY CROSSING
PLIMMERTON
MASTERTON
RAILWAY CROSSING
PORIRUA
UPPER HUTT
RAILWAY CROSSING
CARTERTON
JOHNSONVILLE
CITY
LOWER HUTT
Regional
POPULATION
400,000

BEST
qualified
-and-
HIGHEST-
PAID
workers in the country

POLICY ANALYST = POWER SUIT +
WHITE TRAINERS FOR WALK HOME

THE TERRACE
THERE'S NO OTHER STREET LIKE IT IN THE COUNTRY.
A CORPORATE CANYON OF SKYSCRAPERS PACKED WITH OFFICE WORKERS, MANY OF WHOM ARE GOVERNMENT BUREAUCRATS.
THE PUBLIC SECTOR IS ONE OF THE CITY'S BIGGEST EMPLOYERS AND THE GOVERNMENT LEASES NEARLY
HALF A MILLION SQUARE METRES OF OFFICE SPACE FOR IT'S WORKFORCE. AT NUMBER ONE
THE TERRACE SITS THE TREASURY AND FOR A FEW HUNDRED METRES MORE 'SUITS'
CROWD THE CAFES AND PAVEMENT UNTIL THE CREST OF THE HILL
WHERE ALL THIS FRANTIC ACTIVITY SUBSIDES INTO HISTORIC VILLAS
AND THE BOHEMIA OF ARO VALLEY.

SOUTHERN CROSS
Mi goreng
FRIED NOODLES
Red Bull + Vodka
WELLINGTON MAY NOT HAVE DUNEDIN'S SCARFIE REPUTATION
BUT IT IS BRIMMING WITH STUDENT EXUBERANCE NONE-THE-LESS.
VICTORIA AND MASSEY UNIVERSITIES, AS WELL AS POLYTECHNICS AND WANANGA
HAVE EXPANDED GREATLY IN RECENT TIMES, FUELLED BY THE STUDENT
LOAN SCHEME. SURGING STUDENT DEMAND KEEPS THE CITY'S LANDLORDS
AND HOTELIERS HAPPY.
CORBANS
WHITE LABEL
BYO
Satay Kingdom Café
$$!!
(save)
INDIA PALE ALE
Tui
EXPORT QUALITY
NŌ-DOZ
AWAKENERS
IT'S ALWAYS FREEZIN'!!!
The Big Kumara
SINCE 2001
CIRCLE OF DEATH
(KINGS)
FLAME

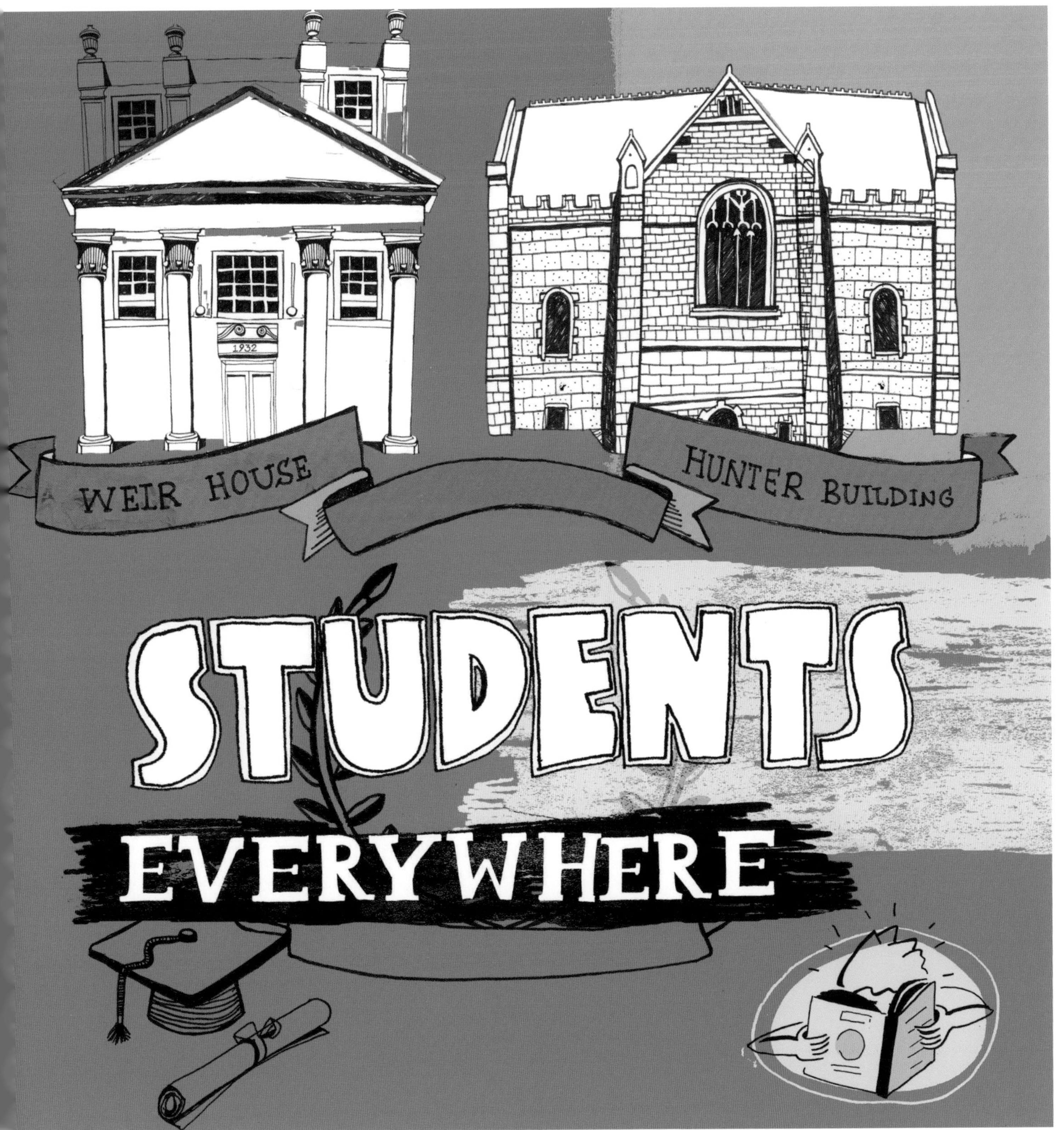
1932
WEIR HOUSE
HUNTER BUILDING
STUDENTS
EVERYWHERE

Matiu Somes Island

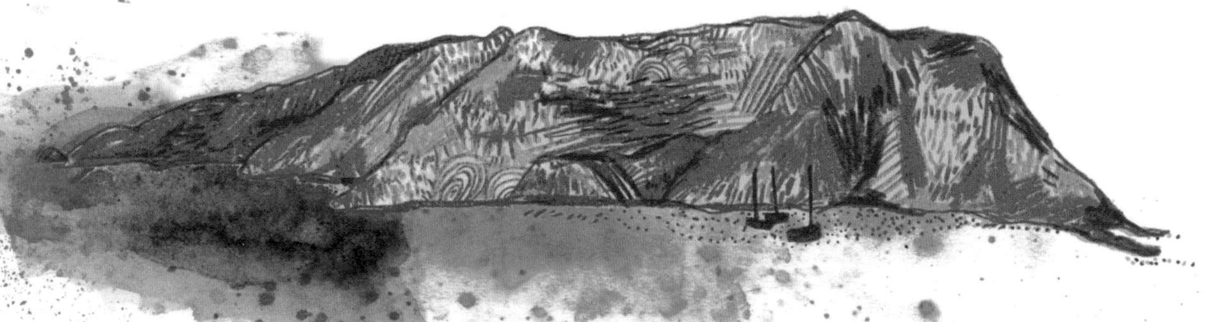

a small island with a big history.

Māori occupied the island for generations.
Matiu Somes Island has served as a human & animal quarantine station, an internment camp, a military fort & since 1995, as a historic reserve.

It has been pest-free since the late 1980s & is a sanctuary for native plants & animals.
The island was given its Māori name by the legendary explorer Kupe 1,000 years ago.
The settlers named it after the New Zealand Company's Deputy Governor, Joseph Somes.
The island enjoys 360 degree views of the harbour & is accessible by a daily ferry service.

R.I.P

TODAY IT IS A TRANQUIL RETIREMENT VILLAGE BUT NOT SO LONG AGO THE WINDY SLOPES OF BERHAMPORE WERE THE SITE OF ONE OF NEW ZEALAND'S MOST CELEBRATED RUGBY VENUES. ATHLETIC PARK WAS ONCE THE HOME OF WELLINGTON RUGBY. IT WAS AN OPEN PARK OVERLOOKING COOK STRAIT AND THE PACIFIC OCEAN. ATHLETIC PARK WAS FAMOUS FOR A VERY STEEP GRANDSTAND, THE MILLARD STAND, WHICH PROVIDED A STUNNING BIRD'S-EYE VIEW OF A GAME BUT

ATHLETIC

USED TO SWAY NOTICEABLY IN THE GUSTY WELLINGTON WINDS. PROPOSALS WERE MADE TO MODERNISE THE GROUNDS IN THE 1980S, BUT IT WAS DECIDED TO BUILD A NEW STADIUM ON THE WATERFRONT. IN 1999 ATHLETIC PARK WAS CLOSED AND REPLACED BY "THE CAKE TIN".

RUGBY
SCOREBOARD
ATHLETIC PARK
SAT
6 JULY
1996
AUSSIE
V
ALL BLACKS
6
43
1961
R.I.P
ATHLETIC PARK
CHATHAM

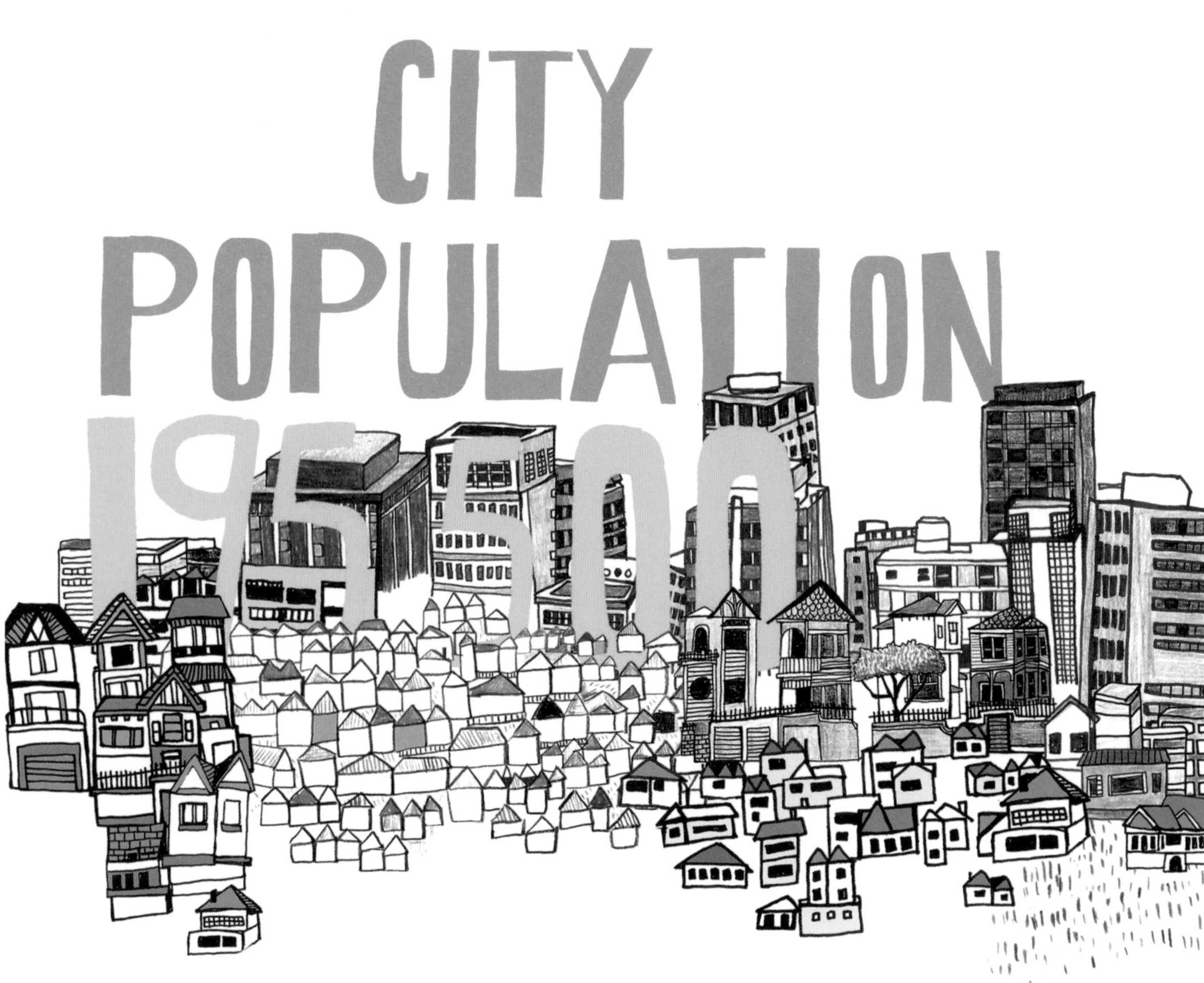
CITY
POPULATION
195500

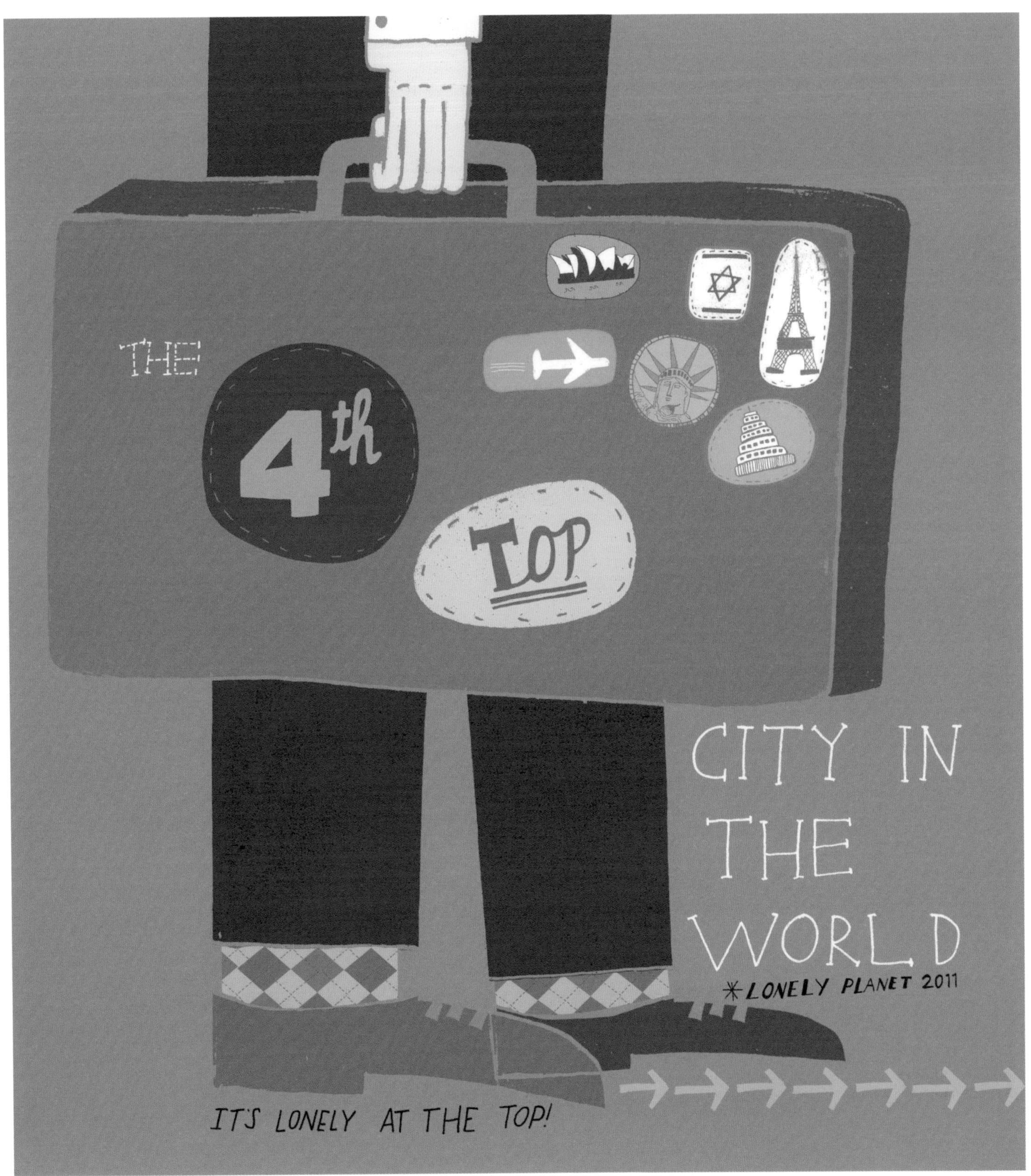
THE
4th
TOP
CITY IN THE WORLD
*LONELY PLANET 2011
IT'S LONELY AT THE TOP!

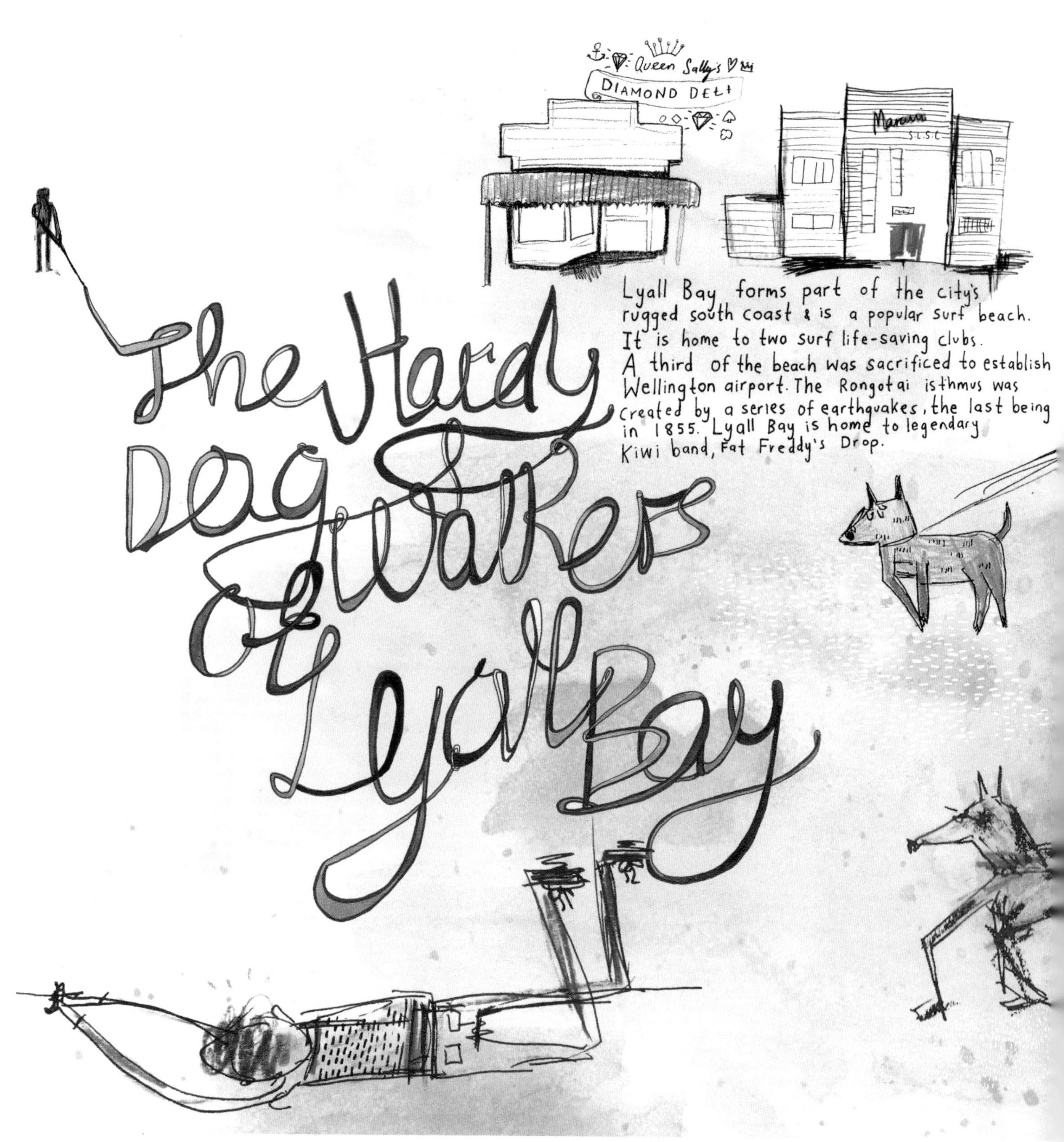
Queen Sally's
DIAMOND DELI
Maranui
S.L.S.C
The Hardy Dog Walkers of Lyall Bay
Lyall Bay forms part of the city's rugged south coast & is a popular surf beach. It is home to two surf life-saving clubs. A third of the beach was sacrificed to establish Wellington airport. The Rongotai isthmus was created by a series of earthquakes, the last being in 1855. Lyall Bay is home to legendary Kiwi band, Fat Freddy's Drop.

Woof Woof
Ruff
(dog exercising area)

TROLLIED!

Wellington's 60 trolley buses are a unique, environmentally-friendly featu of the city's transport system. The trolleys have plied the city's current 50 kilometre network of wires since 1949, although the first service dates back to 1924. For local commuters, the sight of drivers re-attaching trolleypoles that have come off their wires is commonplace. Wellingtonians have strongly opposed various attempts to replace the trolleys with diesel buses and in 2007 a new fleet was commissioned.

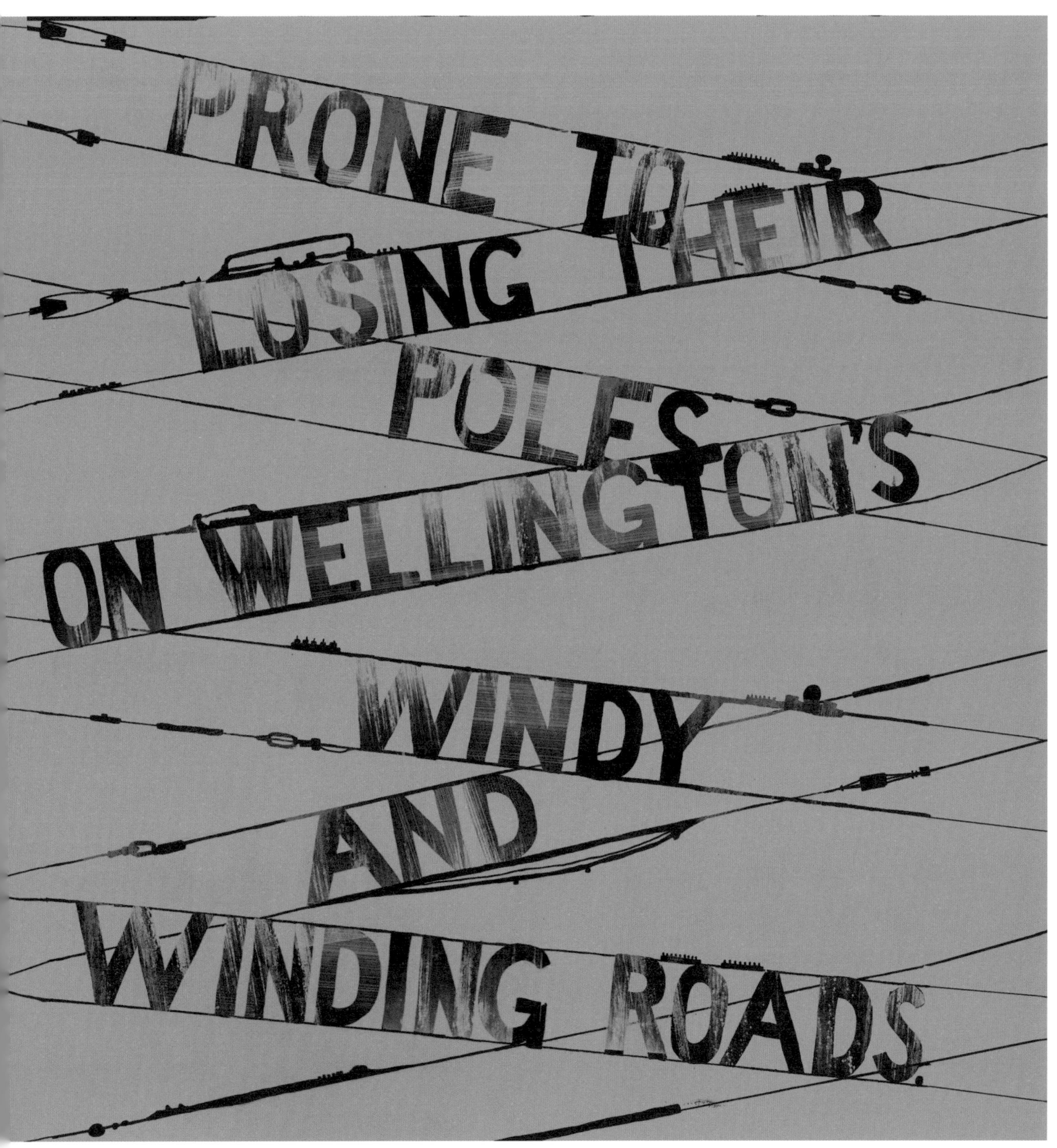
PRONE TO
LOSING THEIR
POLES
ON WELLINGTON'S
WINDY
AND
WINDING ROADS.

Movie
Magic
EMBASSY
PETER
JACKSON

THANKS TO MOVIEMAKER PETER JACKSON, WELLINGTON IS NOW SYNONYMOUS WITH HOLLYWOOD BLOCKBUSTERS. THE HUGELY SUCCESSFUL LORD OF THE RINGS TRILOGY AND KING KONG HAVE PUT NEW ZEALAND ON THE MAP IN A WAY THAT EVEN THE ALL BLACKS CAN'T MATCH. JACKSON'S LOVE OF FANTASY WORLDS HAS ALSO SEEN THE RISE OF AN INTERNATIONALLY RENOWNED SPECIAL EFFECTS INDUSTRY, SPEARHEADED BY RICHARD TAYLOR'S WETA WORKSHOP. A TWO-PART ADAPTATION OF THE HOBBIT LOOKS SURE TO KEEP THE MOMENTUM GOING.

WARDENS, WARDENS EVERYWHERE

WELLINGTON'S ARMY OF PARKING WARDENS GENERATES NEARLY $10 MILLION IN REVENUE EACH YEAR. IN 2009, THIS TIRELESS TROUPE OF FOOTSLOGGERS ISSUED OVER 248,000 TICKETS.

PARKERS BEWARE!

EL MERCADO JUSTO FAIR TRADE
PEOPLES
COMBINED

NEWTOWN, ONE OF WELLINGTON'S FIRST SUBURBS, HAS RETAINED ITS STRONG WORKING CLASS ROOTS DESPITE AN INFLUX OF PROFESSIONALS. MIGRANTS FROM THE PACIFIC, AFRICA, THE MIDDLE EAST AND ELSEWHERE HAVE MADE THE SUBURB ONE OF THE CITY'S MOST INTERESTING AND ETHNICALLY DIVERSE COMMUNITIES. WELLINGTON HOSPITAL WAS BUILT THERE IN 1878, NEW ZEALAND'S OLDEST ZOO BEGAN THERE IN 1906 AND THE CITY'S COLONIAL HERITAGE ENDURES IN NEWTOWN'S WOODEN VILLAS, COTTAGES AND SHOPS.
RIDDIFORD ST
COMBINED

WELLINGTON'S COMPREHENSIVE RAIL NETWORK IS THE ENVY OF OTHER NEW ZEALAND CITIES. WHEN IT WAS COMPLETED IN 1937, THE NEO-GEORGIAN RAILWAY STATION WAS NEW ZEALAND'S LARGEST BUILDING AND A GREAT SOURCE OF CIVIC PRIDE. THE LAND UPON WHICH IT IS BUILT IS RECLAIMED, AND IT WAS THE FIRST MAJOR NEW ZEALAND STRUCTURE TO INCORPORATE EARTHQUAKE RESISTANCE. THE LANDMARK BUILDING REQUIRED 1.75 MILLION BRICKS, PLUS 1,500 TONNES OF DECORATIVE GRANITE AND MARBLE. THE STATION IS A CATEGORY 1 HISTORIC PLACE BUILDING.

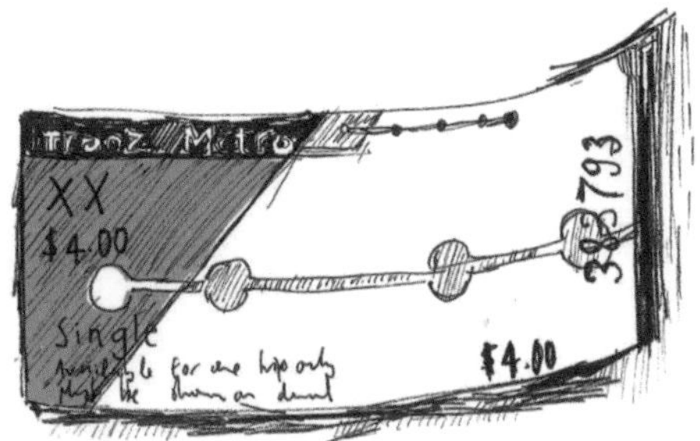

WELLINGTON HARBOUR

WELLINGTON IS BLESSED WITH A SHELTERED, DEEP-WATER HARBOUR SPANNING 70 SQUARE KMS. AROUND 4,200 SHIPS VISIT EACH YEAR INCLUDING NUMEROUS CRUISE SHIPS. THE HARBOUR IS ALSO HOME TO THE INTERISLAND FERRIES, THE PORT NICHOLSON YACHT CLUB, THREE TUGS AND WELLINGTON HARBOUR FERRIES.

QUEEN VICTORIA
EMMA
PILOT
THE DOMINION POST FERRY

Named after an 1840 settler ship, Cuba street is the home of everything left field, late-rising and loose. The inner city thoroughfare, located between Te Aro and Mt Cook, includes a pedestrian MALL and contains an Eclectic mix of boutique stores and op shops selling music, books, clothing, food, SEX products, jewellery, and tattoos. Many of the shop owners are characters worth a visit in their own right and Cuba street's cafes, bars and music venues are the lifeblood of the city's alternative scene. The street contains numerous heritage buildings and has resisted most attempts at modernisation.

GOOD LUCK
Floriditas
KREÜZBERG
SUMMER CAFÉ
Cafe
olive
BATH
HOUSE
FIDELS

lasagna - gluten free
$8.50
VEGAN!!!
YUMMY
goodness
178 CUBA
Midnight Espresso
Matterhorn
The Buddy Holly Story
scopa
SLOW BOAT
RECORDS
Cuba Street
FRUIT MART

The BUCKET FOUNTAIN

Cuba Mall's **Bucket** Fountain, designed in 1969 to mark the **opening** of the mall, has become a Wellington icon, even boasting its own website **and** t-shirts.

A hierarchy of coloured **buckets** fill and splash water into the **shallow** pool below to create a 'Water mobile'.

The artistic merits of the fountain have been hotly disputed over the years, **but** its champions have always won the **day and** in 2003 it was upgraded. It is a favourite **meeting** place for Wellingtonians.

* Elijah Wood

FINDING FAULTS

THE WELLINGTON REGION IS CRISS-CROSSED WITH HUNDREDS OF EARTHQUAKE FAULTLINES AND PRONE TO REGULAR SEISMIC ACTIVITY. SERIOUS EARTHQUAKES, SUCH AS THOSE IN 1848 AND 1855, HAVE SHAPED THE CITY'S TERRAIN AND CHARACTER – THE MASSIVE, 8.2 MAGNITUDE 1855 QUAKE LIFTED THE SEABED BY UP TO TWO METRES AND MUCH OF THE CBD IS BUILT ON THAT RECLAIMED LAND. RISK OF QUAKES ALSO MEANT MOST 19th CENTURY HOUSES AND PUBLIC BUILDINGS WERE CONSTRUCTED OF WOOD. SCIENTISTS SAY THE CITY IS OVERDUE FOR A MAJOR SHAKE AND WELLINGTONIANS HAVE LEARNED TO LIVE WITH THESE DIRE PREDICTIONS.

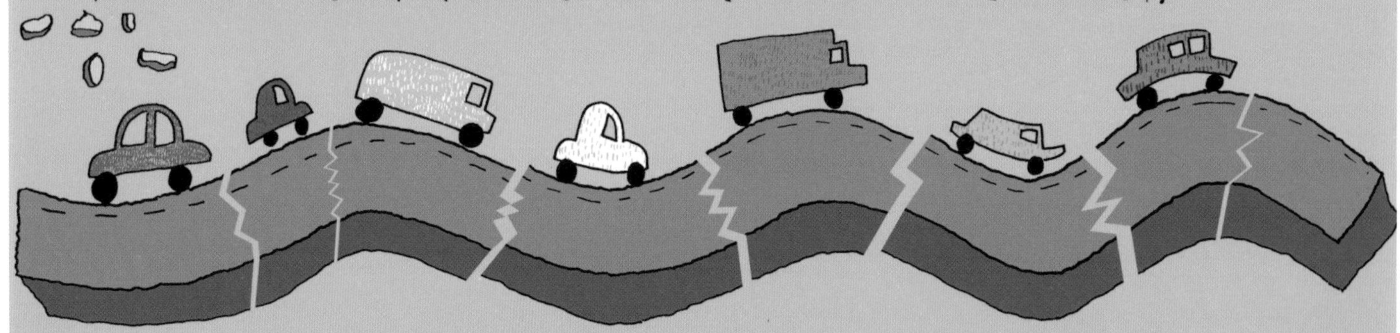

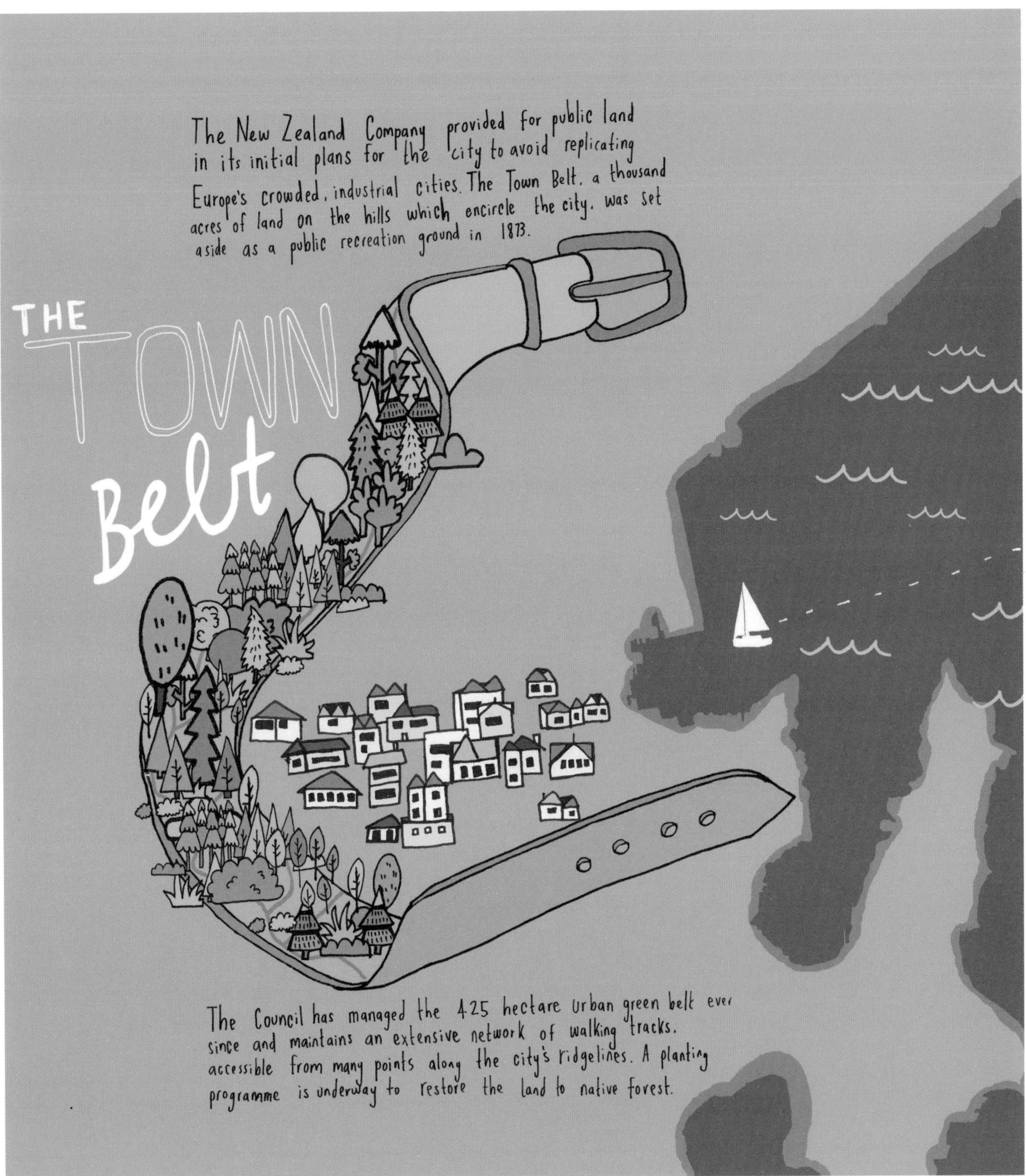
The New Zealand Company provided for public land in its initial plans for the city to avoid replicating Europe's crowded, industrial cities. The Town Belt, a thousand acres of land on the hills which encircle the city, was set aside as a public recreation ground in 1873.
THE TOWN Belt
The Council has managed the 425 hectare urban green belt ever since and maintains an extensive network of walking tracks, accessible from many points along the city's ridgelines. A planting programme is underway to restore the land to native forest.

A good landlord

The Wellington City Council is one of the country's biggest providers of affordable, social housing for those on low incomes. It houses over 4,000 tenants in 40 different housing complexes spread around the city. Over the next 20 years the Council's entire housing portfolio will undergo a multimillion dollar upgrade to modernise the homes and make them safer and warmer.

ONE OF THE MOST AFFORDABLE CITIES IN THE

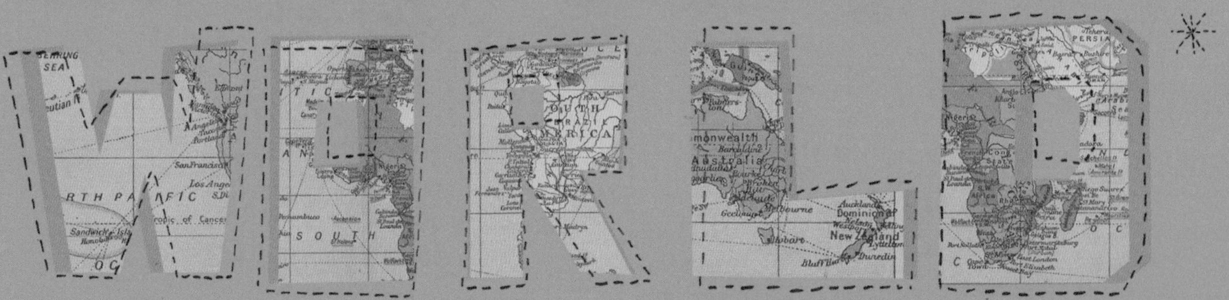

* 138 ARE MORE EXPENSIVE - SO THERE

TE PAPA

OUR PLACE

One of the landmarks of the Wellington waterfront is Te papa Tongarewa, the national museum of New Zealand. Te Papa opened in 1998 and attracts over a million visitors each year. The 36,000 square metre building sits on rubber and steel supports designed to mitigate the effects of any earthquake. The museum is internationally renowned for its interactive, multimedia exhibition spaces.

MANA WHENUA
TE PAPA
TONGAREWA
TOI TE PAPA ART
OUR PLACE
OUR SPACE
britten

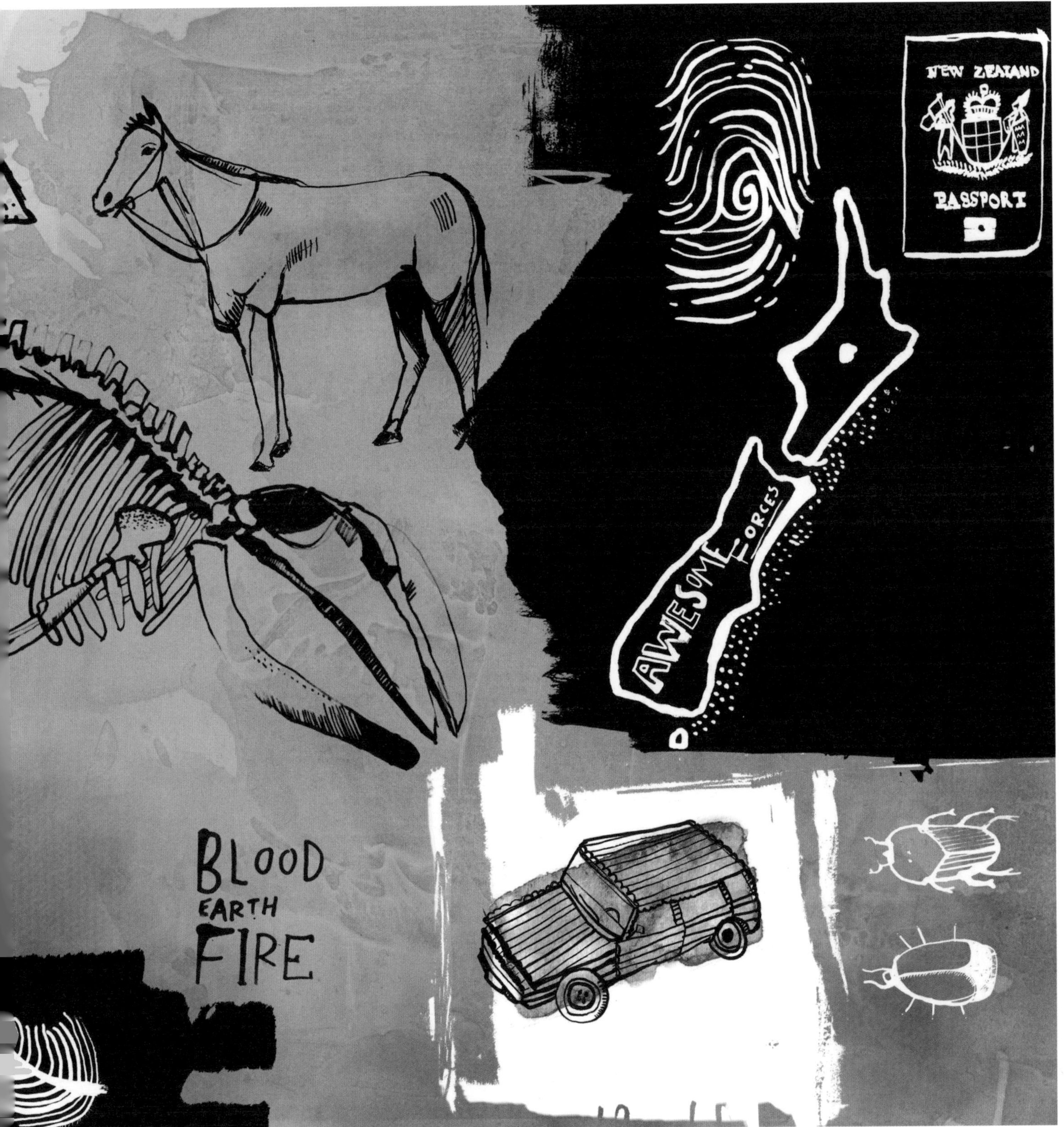
NEW ZEALAND
PASSPORT
AWESOME FORCES
BLOOD
EARTH
FIRE

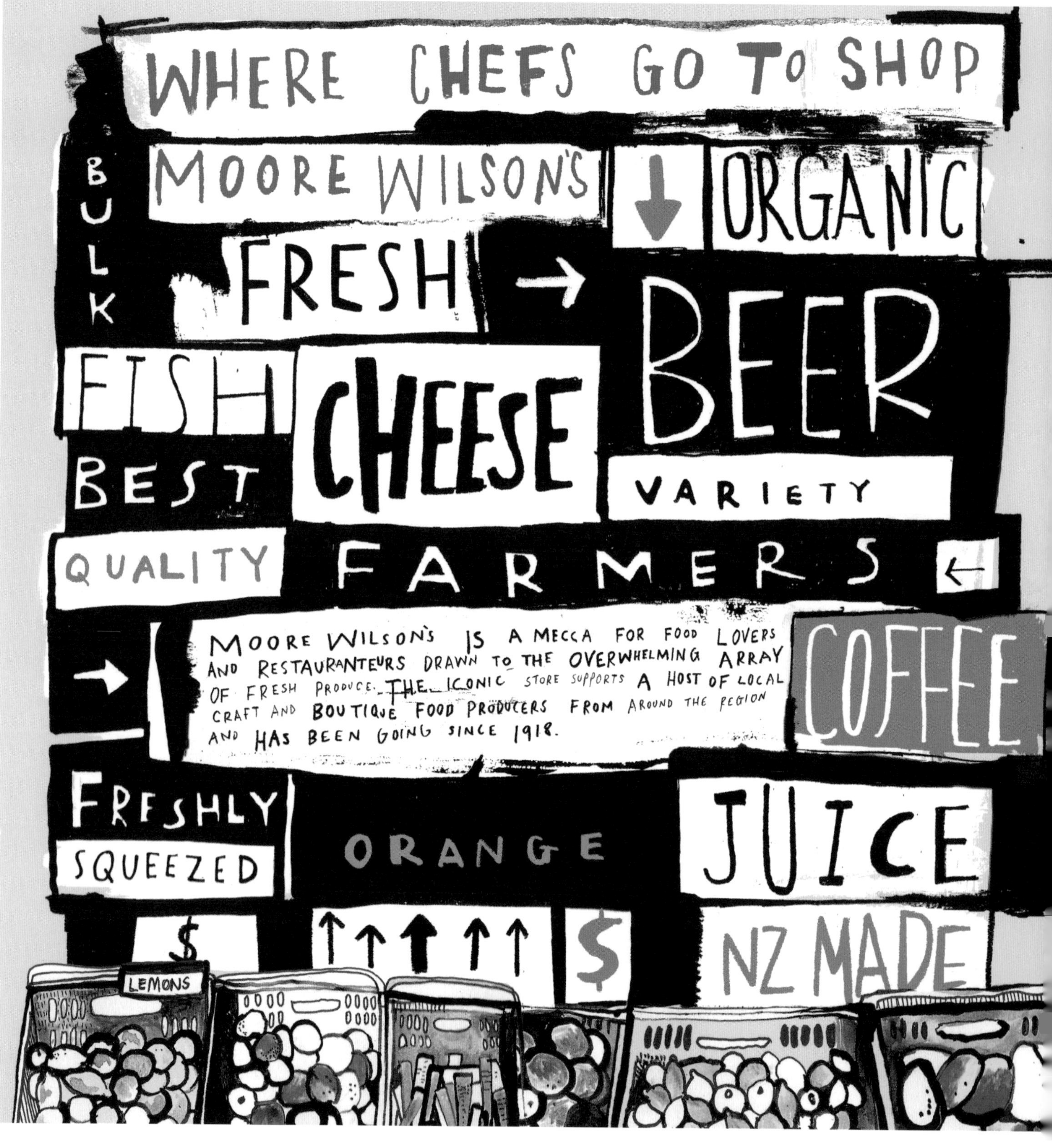

WHERE CHEFS GO TO SHOP
BULK
MOORE WILSON'S
ORGANIC
FRESH
BEER
FISH
CHEESE
BEST
VARIETY
QUALITY
FARMERS
MOORE WILSON'S IS A MECCA FOR FOOD LOVERS AND RESTAURANTEURS DRAWN TO THE OVERWHELMING ARRAY OF FRESH PRODUCE. THE ICONIC STORE SUPPORTS A HOST OF LOCAL CRAFT AND BOUTIQUE FOOD PRODUCERS FROM AROUND THE REGION AND HAS BEEN GOING SINCE 1918.
COFFEE
FRESHLY
SQUEEZED
ORANGE
JUICE
$
$
NZ MADE
LEMONS

DOCKSIDE
LE MÉTROPOLITAIN
Your french bistro
Chippopotamus
CAPITOL
RESTAURANT & BAR
MONSOON
POON
ST JOHNS
Ernesto
LOGAN - BROWN
Restaurant & Bar
DIXON STREET
WELLINGTON
MARTIN BOSLEY'S
BOULCOTT STREET
BISTRO & WINEBAR
BACKBENCHER
Brewery Bar & Restaurant
Fine Dining

THE DISTANCE BETWEEN ANGKOR WAT AND THE CAPITAL GROWS EVER SHORTER THANKS TO AN ABUNDANCE OF CAMBODIAN, VIETNAMESE AND MALAYSIAN NOODLE HOUSES. GENEROUS BOWLS OF STEAMING NOODLE SOUP SUSTAIN WELLINGTONIANS OVER THE LONG WINTER MONTHS. NO NONSENSE DÉCOR ONLY ADDS TO THE CHARM.

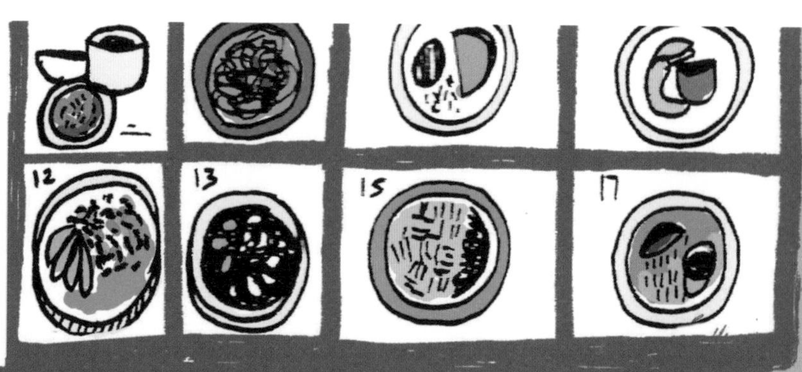

THE NOODLE HOUSE EFFECT

Sunday mornings in Wellington
are made for food lovers.
Foodies on the march
The stalls at farmers markets
such as Harbourside, Hill St
and Victoria Market offer a huge
range of locally-grown
fresh produce
and boutique products.

Summer
at the
DELL
Wellington's Botanical Gardens, set on the hilly slopes of Kelburn and Tinakori, boast 25 hectares of floral displays, plant collections, sculptures and native forest walkways. On balmy (and not so balmy) summer evenings Wellingtonians relax on the Soundshell lawn at the Dell where the City Council hosts concerts.

WAHINE DISASTER
53 dead

275KM/H CYCLONE

CYCLONE GISELLE

ONE OF NEW ZEALAND'S MOST TRAGIC MARITIME DISASTERS, THE SINKING OF THE INTER-ISLAND FERRY WAHINE, WAS CAUSED BY NEW ZEALAND'S WORST RECORDED STORM. ON APRIL 10, 1968, TROPICAL CYCLONE GISELLE FROM THE NORTH COLLIDED WITH A SOUTHERLY ANTARCTIC STORM TO CREATE HURRICANE-STRENGTH WINDS, WITH GUSTS UP TO 275KM/HR. THE WAHINE, CARRYING 734 PASSENGERS AND CREW WAS BATTERED ONTO BARRETT REEF AT THE ENTRANCE OF WELLINGTON HARBOUR AND EVENTUALLY CAPSIZED AT STEEPLE ROCK.

FIFTY-THREE LIVES WERE LOST IN THE RAGING SEAS WHEN THE SHIP WAS ABANDONED. A MEMORIAL ON SEATOUN SHORE MARKS THE TRAGEDY.

BRAVE RESCUERS

10 April

WAHINE MEMORIAL PARK,
SEATOUN

THE CULTURAL CAPITAL

WELLINGTON PRIDES ITSELF ON BEING THE
CREATIVE CAPITAL OF NEW ZEALAND
-HOME OF TE PAPA NATIONAL MUSEUM,
THE SYMPHONY ORCHESTRA, THE INTERNATIONAL
FESTIVAL OF THE ARTS, THE COMEDY AND
FRINGE FESTIVALS, THE WORLD OF WEARABLE
ARTS AND LONG-ESTABLISHED THEATRES
SUCH AS CIRCA, DOWNSTAGE AND BATS. IT'S
THE HOME OF PETER JACKSON AND WETA
WORKSHOP'S FLOURISHING MOVIE EMPIRE AND ALSO
SUPPORTS NUMEROUS ART GALLERIES AND SPECIAL
INTEREST MUSEUMS. FILM FESTIVALS ABOUND.

SHŌGUN
adidas
bnz
350
WGTN DISTRICT
NOTABLE LOCALS
CLUB HOUSE
WELLINGTON

ONCE A WELLINGTONIAN ALWAYS A WELLINGTONIAN

FEELING OVERLOOKED?

TRUNDLING UP THE STEEP TERRAIN BETWEEN LAMBTON QUAY AND UPLAND ROAD, THE CABLE CAR IS BOTH A TOP TOURIST ATTRACTION AND A HANDY SHORTCUT FOR COMMUTERS. DURING THE 628 METRE JOURNEY THERE ARE SPECTACULAR VIEWS, THREE TUNNELS AND SEVERAL STOPS, THE LAST OF WHICH IS THE BOTANICAL GARDENS. THE LINE WAS COMPLETED IN 1902 AS A LINK TO THE NEW SUBDIVISION IN KELBURN. IN 1978 THE OLD CABLE CARS WERE RETIRED AND NEW CARS AND A NEW SYSTEM WERE BUILT.

WELLINGTON CABLE CAR
2
2
2

PENCARROW HEAD

THE WILD AND WINDSWEPT PENCARROW COAST WAS THE SITE OF NUMEROUS SHIPWRECKS, SO NEW ZEALAND'S FIRST **LIGHTHOUSE** WAS ERECTED THERE AT THE EASTERN ENTRANCE TO WELLINGTON HARBOUR IN 1859. TO IMPROVE VISIBILITY IN FOGGY CONDITIONS, ANOTHER TOWER WAS CONSTRUCTED ON THE BEACH IN 1906. PENCARROW HEAD IS NOW A POPULAR WALKING AND MOUNTAIN-BIKING DESTINATION FOR WELLINGTONIANS.

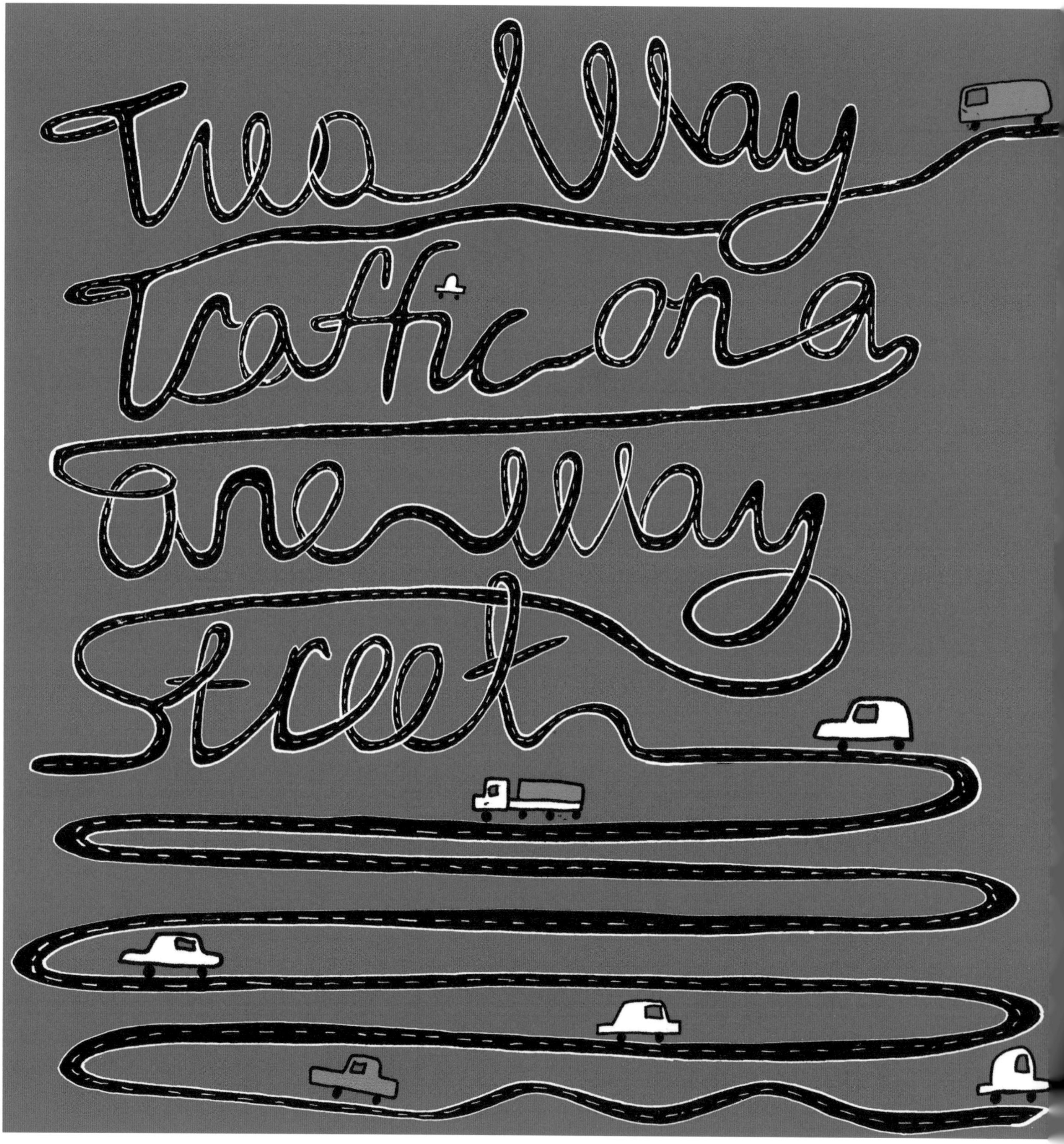

Two Way
Traffic on a
One Way
Street

NO ENTRY
SLOW
NARROW
ROAD

The two lane tunnel was built during the Great Depression and opened on 12 October, 1931. It is 623 metres long and 5 metres high and links Wellington City with the Eastern suburbs. It was the first road tunnel in New Zealand to be mechanically ventilated. 45,000 vehicles pass through it every day, tooting their horns to create a unique Wellington art form.

MOUNT VICTORIA TUNNEL

A SYMPHONY OF BEEPS

THE PORT
WELLINGTON'S BUSY CONTAINER PORT HANDLES 14,000 COMMERCIAL SHIPPING MOVEMENTS A YEAR, MAKING IT A VITAL PART OF NEW ZEALAND'S EXPORT-RELIANT ECONOMY.
MSC

ZEALANDIA
THE KARORI SANCTUARY
THIS AWARD-WINNING ECO ATTRACTION IS A 225 HECTARE, PEST-FREE HAVEN FOR NATIVE BIRDS AND OTHER WILDLIFE.
ALL JUST A STONE'S THROW FROM THE CITY, OR 5 MINUTES AS THE TUI FLIES.

St Gerard's, Mt Vic

COPTHORNE

LOOKING WEST

THE VIEW
FROM MT VIC

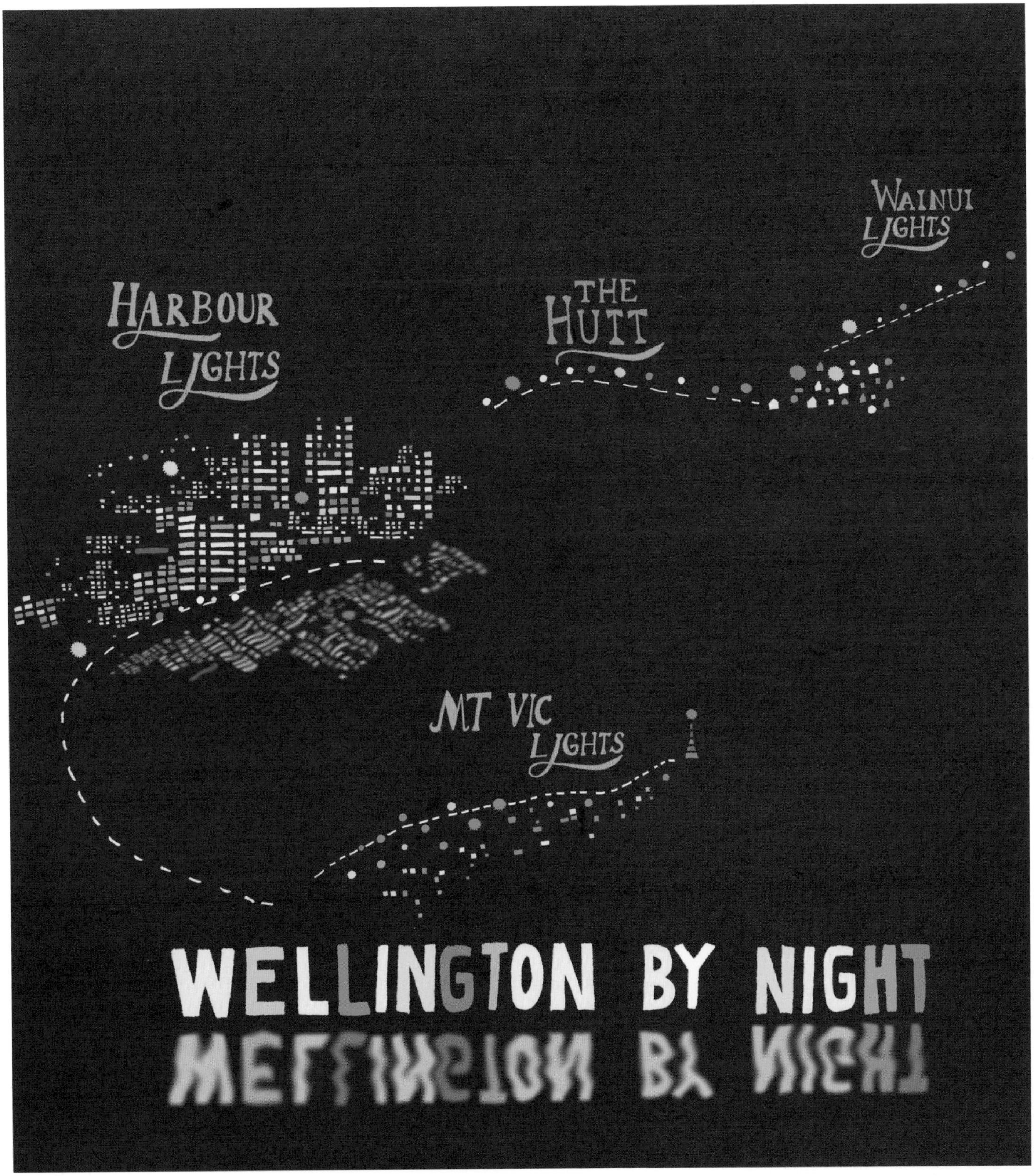

HARBOUR LIGHTS

THE HUTT

WAINUI LIGHTS

MT VIC LIGHTS

WELLINGTON BY NIGHT

SCORCHING BAY

SCORCHING BAY IS THE MOST POPULAR SUNBATHING BEACH IN WELLINGTON. SOFT GOLDEN SAND. DAZZLING TURQUOISE WATERS. A PICTURESQUE BAY SHELTERED FROM THE NORTHERLY. IT'S ALSO A FAVOURITE FOR WALKERS, TRIATHLETES, DIVERS & COFFEE LOVERS.

SET in the RUGGED HILLS of West WELLINGTON, the MAKARA WINDFARM is made up of 62 giant WIND TURBINES. When fully operational, It WILL POWER the equivalent of 73,000 homes. THIRTY THREE Kilometres of access roads were constructed for this 53 SQUARE KILOMETRE site.

a kara Valley
valley
Makara Valley

New Zealand's Finest

MICHAEL FITZSIMONS

Wellington has been home for most of my life, apart from stints in Hawke's Bay and Auckland. Neither the Auckland sprawl, however, nor the climatically advantaged Hawke's Bay got their hooks into me like the Capital.

What is it? The steep hills that enclose us, making us all virtual neighbours? The pearl of a harbour that is so moody and changeable? The turbulent skies and big weather? The dramatic landscape is just the beginning.

Wellington is a friendly place, compact and cosmopolitan. More inclusive than most cities, it attracts all sorts of people and is full of oddities. You can find your niche here.

You can walk from one end of the town to the other in less than an hour. Sometimes I trek home through the town belt that circles the city and head out to Worser Bay, one of the far-flung eastern suburbs. It takes about the same time as a good gym work-out.

Wellington is small in size but big in ideas. Driven indoors, locals have plenty of time to nurture the life of the mind. The city's calendar is full of arts, music and drama. We must be among the world's most dedicated readers and film-goers. We are knee-deep in museums and galleries – I have no idea how the city sustains all this feverish artistic activity but somehow it does.

We're also good at eating and drinking. Our love of fine food is impervious to the recession – restaurants and cafes continue to mushroom. We're addicted to coffee too, drinking more of the stuff per head than they do in New York city.

It never used to be like this. I grew up around the Porirua basin and traveled by train and bus every day to school at the old St Pat's castle on the hill beside the Basin Reserve. The times of those afternoon trains are still inked in my mind – 3.35, 4.00, 4.20, 4.42, 4.55, 5.05, 5.14. The old red units and the 'bone rattler' were my escape from the city. In those days, everyone seemed to be rushing to get out of the place; just a few movie theatres and milk bars stayed open. Courtenay Place was home for the buses and the pigeons, and the waterfront was pretty much deserted.

By the time I joined the throngs of students enjoying a free tertiary education at Victoria University, the city was coming to life. But it is over the last 20 years or so it has transformed into "the coolest little capital in the world," with its bustling public spaces and non-stop events, its crazy mish-mash of waterfront buildings that somehow work, its cafes and bars, its Sevens and WOW festivals, its legions of runners and bikers.

I am a biker of sorts. I head out round the Miramar peninsula, bending my back into the wind, eyes squinting, muscles burning. Other cyclists flash by. Speed and lycra are not my things. I am too busy enjoying the little bays and bush that flourish a stone's throw from the city.

When all is said and done, however, this is Wellington, famous for one thing. We are perched at the southernmost end of an island, and we talk weather incessantly. We moan about it and build sculptures to celebrate it. When the weather turns, a friend of mine heads for the rugged south coast in his van, waiting to welcome the next belter from the south. He says he would spend thousands to travel to weather on the rampage. But he doesn't have to – he lives in Wellington where the weather is a source of wonder as well as a force to be reckoned with.

Of course Wellington is famous for its stunning days too when the rowers are out at dawn and the harbour is as smooth as an egg. What can compare with the sight of Wellington as you sweep down Ngauranga Gorge and out onto the motorway at the harbour's edge?

There it is across the water, shining in the dark pocket of the hills – narrow villas clinging to impossible slopes, a cluster of high rises declaring this is a modern city, New Zealand's finest. A capital city surely?

A Too Long Leaving

NIGEL BECKFORD

I remember my first glimpse of Wellington as the airport bus exploded out the barrel of Mt Victoria tunnel. It was the height of summer and I'd escaped the provinces at last. I was confronted by sheer eccentricity.

There was a cricket ground that doubled as a traffic roundabout, splendidly painted two storied wooden villas perched on precarious slopes, a downtown full of Edwardian masonry sculpted with cake-like precision. There were ridges and hills with more bends and steps than seemed possible and gradients even fit students laboured up like pack mules.

Not far from where I lived lay hairpin bends where buses and fire trucks got stuck. The piles of every house I lived in or visited seemed absolutely shot. Things rolled across floors, doors didn't open and balconies hovered over frightening drops. You didn't need a watch, every bedroom had faster travelling shadows than a sundial - I soon learned sunlight was a precious commodity never to be taken for granted.

I didn't drive then: learning was terrifying. Wellington's one-way system was unforgiving and it was a city of blind corners. Then there was the surf beach where the aircraft roared off a few metres from the break and the flights that felt more like surfing than flying.

The coastline was a collection of alluring bays gleaming with kelp and ice cold water. Togs never felt so inadequate. The southerly gales with their horizontal rain felt brutal to a northerner used to sunny, mild winters – and yet most locals shrugged them off without even a raincoat.

Yes, this town has sent me to some mad places in some testing conditions. I've played soccer on every mud heap the city has to offer. Most are converted landfills. I've bowled into the northerly on its oddly-shaped cricket grounds and emerged red as a beetroot from windburn.

I took part in an inorganic rubbish collection in the eastern suburbs when recycling first came into vogue. The mountainous terrain and the fact that some residents put out entire antique glass houses meant we couldn't walk afterwards.

Fortunately, the compensations have been many. Glorious summer evenings reading books in the town belt, as the last of the sun slides behind the Karori hills. The Oriental Bay of fireworks and promenades. The Cuba Street of gigs, treasured vinyl and late morning rising. And some of the nicest people you could hope to meet anywhere – laid back, smart, savvy, stylish, cheerful, generous, cosmopolitan and willfully oblivious to the city's every fault.

An Italian ambassador once observed that Wellington women dress in black as if they are in mourning. Absurd but true. You could drown in the amount of coffee the place consumes, bolt to international fame on the back of its music scene, witness public sector mandarins turning into hipsters in the space of a drink or break your heart supporting local sports teams who never quite win the one that counts.

At various times, I've been tempted to head somewhere warmer, bigger or busier. But I never have. Instead I've put down roots on an impossibly steep hillside with a cruel lack of afternoon sun. The truth is I've been planning to leave this town for 30 years. And the more I've tried, the longer I've stayed.

Now that's very Wellington.

Sandi and Jess sharpen their pencils...

SANDI MACKECHNIE
JESS LUNNON

_How did you come to be involved in this project?

Jess: It was one of those right place, right time moments.
Sandi: We got asked to do some last minute posters for Nigel's band, he liked it and then it seemed like the next day we were doing the illustrations for the book.

_How did you go about doing the drawings? How do you work as a duo?

Jess: At first we had a list of all the great things/places about Wellington and began sketching. We quickly learnt which illustrations could be done together and which person's drawing style suited an illustration.
Sandi: We have always worked well together. We know what each other are good at. We just try to have fun with what we're doing, the best results often come out of that.

_How do you work up the pictures and make changes?

Jess: Most of the illustrations are hand drawn which allowed us to build up layers separately and work into the same illustrations at one time.
Sandi: Yeah, we ended up getting a massive pile of drawings.
Jess: Working in Photoshop makes it easy to make changes if we need to add different things.
Sandi: We used a mix of media too - colour pencil, ink, pen, photoshop etc.

_How would you describe your illustration style?

Sandi: Fun!
Jess: Changing like the weather.

_What do you like about living in Wellington?

Jess: I love that there is always something to do, that people make the most of the good weather when it appears. It's a friendly place, walking from one side of town to another, you are bound to see someone that you know.
Sandi: The community feel, it's just naturally a really beautiful place, made even better with public spaces, quaint buildings and sculptures. It's got great coffee and great culture.

_What's been the best thing about this project?

Sandi: Working with each other, but also with the writers made it a really rich project and always fun.
Jess: Yeah I agree, and also finding out even more about the wonderful place we live in.

sandidash@gmail.com
jess.lunnon@gmail.com